Countertransference
and
Older Clients

We dedicate this book to Eric Radman, Caroline Preston, our families, our friends, and to all those clients who have taught us so much about our own countertransference feelings and inheritance.

Countertransference
and
Older Clients

edited by
Bonnie Genevay • Renée S. Katz

SAGE PUBLICATIONS
The International Professional Publishers
Newbury Park   London   New Delhi

For information address:

SAGE Publications, Inc.
2455 Teller Road
Newbury Park, California 91320

SAGE Publications Ltd.
6 Bonhill Street
London EC2A 4PU
United Kingdom

SAGE Publications India Pvt. Ltd.
M-32 Market
Greater Kailash I
New Delhi 110 048 India

Printed in the United States of America

Library of Congress Cataloging-in-Publication Data

Main entry under title:

Countertransference and older clients / edited by Bonnie Genevay and
    Renée Katz.
        p. cm.
    Includes bibliographical references.
    ISBN 0-8039-3850-0. — ISBN 0-8039-3851-9 (pbk.)
    1. Social work with the aged—Psychological aspects. 2. Human
services personnel—Psychology. I. Genevay, Bonnie. II. Katz,
Renée.
HV1451.F33 1990
362.6'6—dc20   90-42501
                                                                         CIP

92 93 94 95 10 9 8 7 6 5 4 3 2

Sage Production Editor: Diane S. Foster

Contents

Foreword

Whom do the mourners see? Themselves. Themselves . . .

The American poet Winfield Townley Scott dedicated *Memento,* one of his most painfully acute poems, to the memory of his mother. His grief had already become keen and unrelenting before her death. Mother could no longer recognize him, could no longer remember anything of her long and eventful life. *While you stare down at her long-loved face The nonexistence which shakes you is your own.* . . . Although *Memento* (Scott, 1959) is a lengthy poem, its author needed only one word to express his own reaction to the unresponsive stranger who was also his mother: *terror.*

I have known few clinicians or behavioral scientists who would be as bold as the poet. We may also feel terror, but only as a signal that will rapidly pass from awareness while it is being replaced by one of our high probability response sequences. And so perhaps our momentary inarticulate panic becomes the measured judgment that this person is "not a candidate for therapy." Or perhaps we linger by that display of the latest wonder cosmetic that will peel the wrinkles of incipient age from our brows or restore the youthful appearance of our hair. But perhaps a more cathartic display is what we need—why not explode in rage at those elderly drivers who are clogging up the road?

Alas, these evasions may carry us over fleeting encounters with age, yet fail us abysmally in the long run. The time will come when the social mirror may reflect back to us the same distaste for age that we have been communicating to seniors for years. "Can it be that I am now—one of them? Have I become my terror?"

How valuable it would be to have a clear-eyed, knowing, and honest companion to guide us through this shadow-land. I would have welcomed a book such as this one some 30 years ago when I first started muddling, quite ill- and unprepared to work with aged patients. I welcome it now. The authors have given us what is by far the most extensive and detailed treatment of the counter-transference phenomena that are encountered in the care of elderly men and women. Furthermore I would hurl a copy of this book through the windows of Bureaucrats Anonymous as well as MegaMultivariate Associates. It is not only the helping person— the psychologist, psychiatrist, nurse, recreational therapist, social worker, and so on, who would benefit from an improved understanding of countertransference dynamics. Decision makers, administrators, researchers, and educators are not immune to countertransference effects. In fact, the greater distance between oneself and the client can contribute to extravagant countertransference effects that are less subject to reality constraints.

I think, for example, of the time when I learned that a substantial portion of the food budget for long-term geriatric patients had been—quietly—taken back by the controlling state health care agency. I happened to be the director of that geriatric hospital, and the missing funds came to my attention only when the food services manager expressed concern about being able to purchase enough fruits and vegetables for our nearly 500 aged patients. The "short" of this story was that a budget officer had simply figured that the food account of a geriatric hospital was a nearly invisible, and certainly an insignificant, account from which he could siphon off funds that could be put to better use elsewhere. The "long" of this story came out after he restored the funds with a feeble joke and a shrug of his shoulders. This man could not imagine why the state would want to spend money on useless old people: "I'll tell you the truth—I'd rather be shot than get to be that old!" To this day, he probably has never seen any of the men and women whose health and well-being were endangered by this remote decision. This is hardly an unusual story, but it may help to remind us that the "know-thyself" approach so richly represented throughout this book deserves attention from every thoughtful person, not only professional caregivers.

Nevertheless, the authors have indeed set their sights on the person who provides direct human services to elderly clients. Their respect for both service providers and elderly clients is evident throughout the book. This basic respect—and affection—makes it possible for the authors to go well beyond the platitudinous. They think that you and I really care about what we are doing, and that we are willing to face some uncomfortable challenges and revelations when necessary to reach our potential. In some respects, then, this is a tough little book. For example, perhaps you and I would prefer not to take the self-awareness quiz in Chapter 5—but I bet we do it anyway, and learn from it! Similarly, we might feel a little uneasy about the suggestion that whether or not a client commits suicide could depend on how we work with our own emotional reactions. And yet it is probable that this very uneasiness will impel us to examine the therapist-client interaction. These are but two of many examples. Our individual encounters with countertransference dynamics may well generate some bumps, wobbles, and sudden stops as we make our way through the book, but this will only contribute to making the journey all the more eventful and instructive.

One more observation, please: This book reminds time and again of the distinctive personal bonds that can be formed between a person who has weathered so many storms and tribulations of the human soul, and a person for whom age is still terra incognito. Just as Freud wrote to Einstein about the need to love ourself in the other person and the other person in our self (Freud & Einstein, 1933), so the present book encourages us to appreciate the youth in the aged person, and the aged person in the youth.

References

Freud, S., & Einstein, Albert. (1933). *Why War?* Chicago: Chicago Institute for Psychoanalysis.
Scott, W. T. (1959). *Scrimshaw* (pp. 19-26). New York: Macmillan.

—Robert Kastenbaum, Ph.D.

Acknowledgement

We gratefully acknowledge the following people who have inspired, guided, and supported us in our shared journey to explore being fully human and fully professional at the same time: Eric Radman, Robert Kastenbaum, Judy McLean, and Marquita Flemming, without whom this book would never have been born, and especially our chapter authors, who gave unstintingly of their time, energy, and expertise to birth this project.

Bonnie Genevay
Renée S. Katz

Introduction

This is a book about how our feelings about aging and loss, and about disability and death affect our work with older people. It is addressed to all who work with old and dying people, and to those who work with younger people who have become "instantly old" due to disability. This includes case managers, pharmacists, aides, social workers, psychiatrists, ministers, hospital chaplains, nurses, outreach workers, physicians, occupational therapists, physical therapists, volunteers, attorneys, psychologists, and the staff members of all disciplines in senior centers, adult day centers, adult foster homes, retirement homes, and nursing homes.

In our work with older people and their families, we come face to face with thoughts, memories, feelings, and unresolved issues from our own lives. As professionals in the field of gerontology, many of us have not been sensitized to see our own real reactions and feelings towards clients and patients, and have experienced an impermeable membrane between personal and professional behaviors. We have been trained to deny that each of us faces loss, disability, and dying—so that we can focus on the *client's* needs. But this membrane is permeable! We can connect our feelings and experiences with those of the patients and clients we serve; and we can provide better diagnosis and treatment in the process. Out of our own observations of ourselves and our aging families, we can become more effective professionals and more sensitive to the people we help.

Our concept of countertransference—the personal-professional connection—will be defined and demonstrated throughout the book. Very simply put, countertransference is the powerful linkage between helpers' personal feelings and their professional interventions and behaviors. *Transference* describes the feelings clients have about us, which we think we can handle easily because it is their problem. *Countertransference* means all the feelings we have about clients. These feelings are harder to handle because we are the ones on the "hot seat."

Using our conceptual framework of countertransference, we pinpoint such issues as how we "overhelp" and "underhelp" some clients because of our feelings rather than their conditions; how personal and family biases contribute to inappropriate diagnosis, referral, and treatment; how professional stress and burnout occur when countertransference is overlooked; how we happen to prolong service with some clients and terminate others too soon; how we may ignore essential data such as substance and other abuse; how we deny the lifelong sexual habits and intimacy needs of older people when we find them threatening to us; and how our fears of AIDS, death, and suicide keep us from providing effective support and treatment.

We would like to let the reader in on the process of creating this book, for it very much relates to the content of the book and has been an extraordinary process in its own right. The book began with a phone call from Renée to Bonnie, who was an old friend and Renée's first teacher of Aging and Human Development at the University of Washington in 1978. Renée suggested co-writing an article on countertransference for *Generations*, the Journal of the American Society on Aging. This article was written rather quickly, over the telephone between Seattle and San Francisco, and became "Older People, Dying and Countertransference," which was published in the Spring, 1987 issue of *Generations.*

It seemed quite natural for us to then say to each other, "This is good stuff—maybe it should be a book!" The book was reinforced by the continual usage of the article as a handout in the training and teaching we have both done across the country since 1987. The most common response to the article and to the training with professionals in gerontology has been, "I'm so glad you wrote about countertransference; there isn't much in the literature; I don't receive much support in my practice about my own personal-professional aging and dying issues."

Heartened by this response, we proceeded to locate the best chapter authors in their respective fields; we engaged in voluminous correspondence to select the best editor and publishing house for this book; and edited and re-edited the chapters again and again. We often thought we were being crystal clear with our chapter authors, and we weren't. We believed our concept of countertransference was being communicated, and it wasn't. From the beginning this book was a totally shared project—*our* baby, co-parented as equally as we knew how. No decision was made without a long-distance telephone conversation or the exchange of written material. Sometimes Renée would do more when Bonnie was overwhelmed with training and traveling, and sometimes Bonnie would do more when Renée had an unbelievably heavy schedule. Whatever was occurring in our personal and professional lives, never—in our naiveté—did it occur to us to wonder who would be "first author" or whose name would go first on the cover.

In the spring of 1990, when Marquita Flemming, our editor at SAGE, made it very clear that *we'd* have to make this decision because it was *our* book, we were caught short. An amazing honesty between us—which had always been there—deepened. We talked about our feelings toward each other personally first, and then feelings toward ourselves professionally. Marquita was wonderful in her innovative and creative support of all that could be done graphically and structurally to show our strongly felt co-authorship.

We agreed that we didn't want to defer to each other because "Bonnie was older and might die sooner," or because "Renée had a Ph.D. and Bonnie 'only' had a Master's degree." We came out of long talks with great mutual respect for the fact that we were two strong and stubborn professionals, and two powerful women. We discovered we were unwilling to play "you go first, you need it worse" and other games. We asked each other what was at stake, and agreed that it was not a great deal more than our egos. And we struggled with how to communicate this exciting, joyful, difficult, demanding shared creatorship with our readers. For—make no mistake—this *is* a struggle with countertransference we're describing to you! The birth of this book is greatly bound up with our feelings toward each other personally and professionally. And our feelings affect the end product just as surely as *your* personal and professional feelings affect your end products—the diagnosis, treatment and services delivered to your clients, patients, and their families.

We talked to each other a great deal and came up with many schemes to show equality of authorship. All we can finally say is that the honesty—which we may sometimes like when it's not too close, or *not* like when it gets in the way of our treasured blindspots—has been worth it all. Enormous mutual respect has been one of the fruits of our collaboration. This book has been conceived, brought through long labor (it's felt like being pregnant with an elephant at times), and birthed *equally* between Renée Katz and Bonnie Genevay.

We share this process with you because it represents the same kind of professional countertransference that exists between you and your supervisees, you and your colleagues, you and your supervisors, and you and your organizations.

We hope that you will read this book with "new glasses" that screen out old values and attitudes that no longer serve you, and with a strong regard for the excellent professional skills you have already acquired. This book is designed to help you add one more skill: awareness of your countertransference issues and the ability to take appropriate action when they arise. We invite you to discover how your own aging, disability, and dying—and those of your family—connect with the work you are doing. If you choose to confront these potent issues, we believe that your work will be enhanced and your spirit enriched—and that your clients and patients will be the winners.

Renée S. Katz
Bonnie Genevay

1

Using Our Emotional Reactions to Older Clients: A Working Theory

RENÉE S. KATZ

The Personal-Professional Connection

Helping professionals often have intense reactions to the people with whom we work. These arise from our personal experience of aging and loss in ourselves, in our family members, and in other significant people in our lives. These reactions tell us that there is a personal and professional interface, an invisible connection between our own life developmental tasks and issues and our professional interventions and behaviors. In our work with aging clients, we can deny these thoughts and feelings, or we can choose to consult them. When identified, these countertransference reactions provide useful data for diagnosis and intervention (Beitman, 1983; Dunkel & Hatfield, 1986; Katz & Genevay, 1987). If we can

17

manage rather than deny our own fears and feelings, we cannot help but be more effective with clients.

Countertransference was first defined by Freud as an unconscious process involving the arousal of the analyst's unresolved conflicts and problems (Freud, 1959a). In this classical definition, countertransference was regarded as an obstacle to the psychoanalytic treatment process, a blind spot that the analyst had to overcome and eliminate in order to function effectively (Freud, 1959b). Over the years, however, the definition of countertransference has broadened to include the *totality* of feelings experienced by the therapist toward the client—whether conscious or unconscious, whether prompted by the client or by events in the therapist's own life (Langs, 1983; Dunkel & Hatfield, 1986). The countertransference process is regarded as an appropriate, natural emotional response of positive value (Kernberg, 1965; Racker, 1968). It is an important therapeutic tool (Heimann, 1950; Little, 1951); the basis for empathy and for deeper understanding of both the older client's and the helper's own processes (Peabody & Gelso, 1982). Sandler, Cristopher, and Holder (1973) have suggested that work with countertransference issues be extended beyond strict psychoanalytic treatment. We, too, regard an understanding of the countertransference process as a useful element in *any* therapeutic relationship. We believe that as helping professionals in the fields of aging, dying, and disability, we are inevitably affected by the interface between our own aging processes, our families' aging, and that of the people with whom we work. The aging, disabled, and dying family members of the practitioner who is working with old, disabled, and dying clients are a critical part of his or her countertransference responses, thus creating a Triangle of Countertransference (see Figure 1.1).

Consulting our countertransference reactions means being honest with ourselves about our personal Triangle of Countertransference and our difficulties in moving through our own life cycles. The key to the acknowledgment of countertransference lies in feelings—*ours*.

Countertransference provides an extraordinary opportunity for the helping person to look at his or her own distance from potential and real losses, disability, aging, and death, in order to be a more competent helper. The benefits of pursuing this complex and deeply personal journey are invaluable to both helper and client.

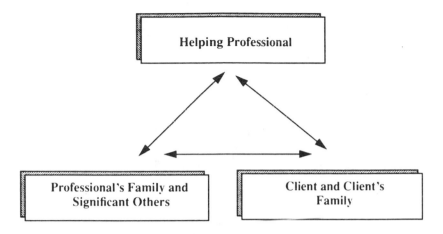

Figure 1.1. Triangle of Countertransference

Acknowledging countertransference feelings can help us come to a deeper understanding and appreciation for each person's and each family's own processes. When we can face our own intense emotional reactions and their meanings without feeling too threatened, we can then engage in a responsive therapeutic relationship that enables us to grow as persons and as professional helpers. By understanding and integrating our feelings into our work, we not only have the potential for helping our clients, but we also benefit: our clients and patients serve as models helping us face our own inevitable aging, losses, and eventual death with less fear.

To understand the potential of our emotional reactions, it is useful to step back and look at the context in which we all move through our own life journeys as we work with our aging clients.

Ageism

Each human being is unique, unprecedented, but to make that elegant expression meaningful, society must be so organized that people can continue to grow to the very end of life. (Butler, 1975, p. 385)

We, however, live in a society fueled by the media's worship of youth and beauty. We are obsessed with a fast-paced lifestyle. We emphasize efficiency and productivity; we promulgate youthful appearance, activity, and independence as standards of personal worth (Hendricks & Hendricks, 1977). Young, in America, is beautiful, good, independent, and powerful; old is worthless, sexless, senile, ill, isolated, and lonely (Levin & Levin, 1980). Instead of regarding old age as a valuable, final culmination of the life cycle, our society promotes a stereotypical view of aging as less than normal—a stigma involving negative references to older people based on their age status alone.

Rosow (1976) explains that America perpetuates a youth-oriented culture (at the expense of our value for old age and aging) because those

> institutionalized forces that typically support the position of old people in simpler societies are inimical to them in our own. Paradoxically, our productivity is too high and our mutual dependence too low. We are too wealthy as a nation and too self-sufficient as individuals to need older people, and the significant functions open to them are shrinking. This both reflects and reinforces other established cultural values, such as our greater concern for the young . . . (p. 7)

Further, ageism, like sexism or racism, may serve as a protection against fears involving helplessness, vulnerability, and inferiority (Katz, 1988). By projecting negative attributes onto older people, and by avoiding discussion of or contact with the aging process, we may use ageism to protect our own self-esteem and perceived status in life when we are younger. Ageism ultimately protects a youth-oriented society from its anxiety about death, illness, and loss of meaning in life (Katz, 1988; Levin & Levin, 1980).

Aging

Despite our society's continuing avoidance of aging, helping professionals are perhaps most acutely aware of and more frequently confronted with unusual, "non-normative" age changes. Our work with individuals and families who are facing life crises and developmental turning points challenges us—in fact, forces us—to re-define the experience of aging in completely new, uncharted ways.

At any given stage of development, Havighurst (1973) notes, we each carry with us our own personalized conception of human nature, a commonsense notion about the way people are. We don't necessarily verbalize our personal theories, but they are implied in all our actions. We begin developing our model early in life. By late adolescence, we have a personal schema of normal human development that we modify only slightly as we meet new people or situations that don't quite fit.

Yet, what happens when our schema of "normal" development, or progress through the lifecycle, is confronted with an inexplicable reality? Our respected colleague, 38 years old, is diagnosed with AIDS. Our best friend's daughter, 15 years of age, is the victim of a car accident, left paralyzed from the neck down. Our favorite patient is diagnosed with terminal cancer. Our beloved father, an independent, vibrant man, is diagnosed with Alzheimer's disease at age fifty. What happens *then* to our conceptualization of life and living? Of growing up and growing old? What happens to our assumptions about aging, loss, and death?

By virtue of our work alone, we are compelled to ask: What does "aging" mean? When does it begin? How do we measure it or gauge it? And, more profoundly, how can we accept it and live with it? The answers to these questions have eluded social scientists for years and the debates continue. We inevitably obtain different answers to the questions of aging depending on who we talk to! Health and medical professionals, for instance, profess a bio-physiological definition, stressing changes in the structure and functions of various body parts. Psychologists, social workers, teachers, and other psycho-socially oriented professionals espouse socio-behavioral, emotional, or cognitive maturation and development as markers of aging. Still others vie for a view of aging that encompasses a series of spiritual encounters and progressions involving the growth and decline of the psyche. All, however, undoubtedly agree that chronological (calendar) age alone is simply insufficient to describe the aging process (Botwinick, 1984; Karp & Yoels, 1982).

Our task then is to make some sense of the meaning of aging as it impacts each of us individually, familially, and professionally. For the purposes of this book, we have found it useful to draw from the theories of Havighurst (1972), Neugarten (1969), Kastenbaum (1975), Atchley (1975), and Filipp and Klauer (1986).

Developing a Working Theory of Aging

As early as 1948, Havighurst began to describe human development and aging in terms of the interaction between biological and social constraints, demands, and opportunities. Neugarten (Neugarten, Moore, & Lowe, 1965) followed suit with the concept of "Social Time" or, in Atchley's (1975) words, "Biographical Time"—the way in which an individual experiences his or her own life span.

In our conceptualizations of aging (see Figure 1.2, Triangle of the Aging Experience), the "Social Time Clock" (Neugarten & Datan, 1973) consists of a tripartite, interactive model involving: (1) movement through the life cycle, (2) place in society, and (3) subjective interpretation of age (Karp & Yoels, 1982).

Life events as well as age-linked biological opportunities (Movement Through the Life Cycle) interact with and are influenced by social expectations, behaviors, and age-related norms (Place in Society). At age six, for example, cognitive and biological development make it possible for a child to attend school. At the same time, society has come to expect, and even mandate, school attendance. Thus, age six becomes a social marker of readiness for education, and children are expected to fulfill their age-related social roles of students. Adjusting to and fulfilling the tasks inherent in the role of student thus become part of the age-linked developmental tasks to be accomplished at this stage of the life cycle.

In addition, at any age, our social comparisons with others in our environment or social group will impact our attitudes toward our identity, toward our self-esteem *and* toward our personal conceptions of aging. This is "Subjective Interpretation," or as Neugarten describes it, an awareness of being "on-time" or "off-time."

> The age grade system institutionalizes cultural values and constitutes a social system that shapes the life cycle. Every society has a system of social expectations regarding age-appropriate behavior, and these expectations are internalized as the individual grows up . . . and moves from one age stratum to the next. (Neugarten & Datan, 1973, p. 59)

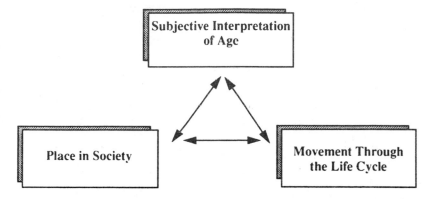

Figure 1.2. Triangle of the Aging Experience

Our society has age-related standards and timetables along the life course—times when we are expected to learn, work, commit to a life partner, raise a family, retire, grow sick, even die (Neugarten & Datan, 1973). Although fluctuations and variations occur, age-linked demands that are socially prescribed seem to result in certain consistent, normative patterns and sequences throughout the life cycle (Atchley, 1975).

At age 30, for instance, we might be en route to a career or life work; we might be establishing long-term commitments to relationships and family. We probably have a good idea of where we stand vis-à-vis the social time clock (Neugarten & Datan, 1973). We might even describe ourselves in terms of our time clock as "late bloomers" or "early starters," or as "having a family later than usual."

Ultimately, then, the Triangle of the Aging Experience—our personal interpretation of ourselves and others in the environment, our location in the life course, and our socially mandated norms, roles, and expectations—gives meaning to and defines our personal concepts of aging. If there is a disparity between actual and expected functioning, if our social time clock has run amuck, then our perceptions of age or advancing years may undergo an unexpected metamorphosis. Filipp and Klauer (1986) point out that

The adoption of new social roles, included in many major life transitions, has been seen as providing the individual with changes in social feedback which might force him or her to integrate new, often discrepant information in the self-concept . . . life events often lead to a change in one's reference groups, which might result in a profound change in . . . self-[reference] . . . (pp. 197-198)

When a 21-year-old is given three months to live, or when a 40-year-old's biological integrity is not maintained—as occurs in multiple sclerosis—these unexpected circumstances catapult the individual into an unprecedented location in the life course. Suddenly they are "young" in life experience, but "old" in functional status. They are likely, in fact, to experience all the symptoms we typically associate with old age: stigma, deprivation, and isolation; loss of roles, relationships, health, and money; perhaps loss of opportunities to fulfill personal life goals.

Any major, unanticipated disruption in the life cycle can threaten to reshape the entire life course of the people with whom we work. As practitioners and helpers in all disciplines, we are undoubtedly sought out at precisely those times when psychological distress and anxiety escalate. We may see our clients' goals and expectations shatter; we may watch their customary coping methods deteriorate; we may feel their anxiety deeply and personally; we may experience their pain in ways inexplicable to ourselves.

This book is precisely about confronting these developmental issues—in our clients and their families, in our colleagues, in our families and close friends, and in ourselves. Together we will examine the meanings and contexts of aging, and the impact of these meanings on our work lives and on our personal lives.

The triangle of countertransference (Figure 1.1) and the triangle of aging (Figure 1.2) are the conceptual vehicles we offer you as a framework for looking at dementia, aging, caregiving, nursing home placement, case management, substance abuse and co-dependency, intimacy and sexuality, suicide, AIDS and HIV, disability, and death.

References

Atchley, R. C. (1975). The life course, age grading and age-linked demands for decision-making. In N. Datan & L. H. Ginsberg (Eds.), *Life-span developmental psychology: Normative life crises* (pp. 261-277). New York: Academic Press.

Beitman, G. (1983). Categories of counter-transference. *Journal of Operational Psychiatry, 14*(2), 91-98.

Botwinick, J. (1984). *Aging and behavior.* New York: Springer.

Butler, R. N. (1975). *Why survive? Being old in America.* New York: Harper & Row.

Dunkel, J., & Hatfield, S. (1986, March-April). Countertransference issues in working with persons with AIDS. *Social Work,* 114-117.

Filipp, S., & Klauer, T. (1986). Conceptions of self over the life span: reflections on the dialectics of change. In M. M. Baltes & P. B. Baltes (Eds.), *The psychology of control and aging* (pp. 180-201). New Jersey: Lawrence Erlbaum.

Freud, S. (1959a). The future prospects of psychoanalytic therapy. In E. Jones (Ed.), *Collected papers of Sigmund Freud* (Vol. 2, pp. 285-286). New York: Basic Books. (Original work published in 1910.)

Freud, S. (1959b). Recommendations for physicians on the psychoanalysis method of treatment. In E. Jones (Ed.), *Collected papers of Sigmund Freud* (Vol. 2, pp. 323-333). New York: Basic Books. (Original work published in 1912.)

Havighurst, R. J. (1972). *Developmental tasks and education.* New York: David McKay.

Havighurst, R. J. (1973). The history of developmental psychology: socialization and personality development through the lifespan. In P. B. Baltes & K. W. Schaie (Eds.), *Life-span developmental psychology: Personality and socialization* (p. 26). New York: Academic Press.

Heimann, P. (1950). On countertransference. *International Journal of Psycho-Analysis, 31,* 81-84.

Hendricks, J., & Hendricks, C. (1977). *Aging in mass society: Myths and realities.* Cambridge, MA: Wenthrop.

Karp, D. A., & Yoels, W. C. (1982). *Experiencing the life cycle: A social psychology of aging.* Springfield, IL: Charles C. Thomas.

Kastenbaum, R. (1975). Is death a life crisis? On the confrontation with death in theory and practice. In N. Datan & L. H. Ginsberg (Eds.), *Life-span developmental psychology: Normative life crises.* New York: Academic Press.

Katz, R. S. (1988). *Personality trait correlates of attitudes toward aging.* Unpublished doctoral dissertation, California School of Professional Psychology, Berkeley.

Katz, R. S., & Genevay, B. (1987, Spring). Older people, dying and countertransference. *Generations,* pp. 28-32.

Kernberg, O. (1965). Notes on countertransference. *Journal of the American Psychoanalytic Association, 13,* 38-56.

Langs, R. (1983). Therapists' reactions to the patient. *The technique of psychoanalytic psychotherapy* (Vol. 2). New York: Jason Aronson.

Levin, J., & Levin, W. C. (1980). *Ageism: Prejudice and discrimination against the elderly.* Belmont, CA: Wadsworth.

Little, M. (1951). Countertransference and the patient's response to it. *International Journal of Psycho-Analysis, 32,* 32-40.

Neugarten, B. L. (1969). Continuities and discontinuities of psychological issues into adult life. *Human Development, 12,* 121-130.

Neugarten, B. L., & Datan, N. (1973). Sociological perspectives on the life cycle. In P. B. Baltes & K. W. Schaie (Eds.), *Life-span developmental psychology: personality and socialization* (pp. 53-71). New York: Academic Press.

Neugarten, B. L., Moore, J. W., & Lowe, J. C. (1965). Age norms, age constraints and adult socialization. *American Journal of Sociology, 70,* 710-717.

Peabody, S. A., & Gelso, C. J. (1982). Countertransference and empathy: the complex relationship between two divergent concepts in counseling. *Journal of Counseling Psychology. 29*(3), 240-245.

Rosow, I. (1976). *Socialization to old age.* Berkeley, CA: University of California Press.

Racker, H. (1968). *Transference and countertransference.* New York: International Universities Press.

Sandler, J., Cristopher, D., & Holder, A. (1973). *The patient and the analyst.* New York: International Universities Press.

2

Creating a More Humane Dying

BONNIE GENEVAY

When I was seven years old my grandmother died. . . . *I hated* her for
dying and leaving *me*; and I hated my mother and father for letting it
happen. . . . I (finally) figured out that I thought my grandmother
died because I was a kid and didn't know enough to save her. So . . .
I went into nursing to try to stop separation . . . in order to stop
separation in nursing I would have had to stop death . . . (Gino, 1982,
pp. 19, 21, 350-351)

Memories, feelings, and issues related to the dying of our own
grandparents, siblings, and other significant people in our lives
impact the work we do with the dying. The threat of our own
mortality—the ultimate loss of ourselves—also affects the help we
give.

I encourage helpers of all disciplines to confront countertransference responses as part of appropriate professional behavior.

This makes possible the kind of therapeutic intervention that enables the dying to plan for and face their mortality with dignity and integrity, with power and choice. Confronting this personal-professional connection means being clear with ourselves about our values, and it means separating our clients and patients from ourselves and our family experiences with dying. This context includes dying people of all ages, but it particularly concerns older people, who suffer from our societal bias that it's all right to die as long as you are old but not all right if you are young (see Chapter 1). Dying is sometimes a long, slow process, not simply the last three days or three weeks of life, as in the following example:

> I think Mom started actively dying the day she was sure (my Dad) wasn't going to "make it," and that was some six months before he actually did die. Her dying process took seven years and it made all the stops along the way . . . Parkinson's, emphysema, osteoporosis. (Watt, 1988, p. 2.)

With this concept of dying in mind, this chapter will address: (1) denial and the helping role; (2) honesty as a valid therapeutic approach; (3) helplessness and the professional role; and (4) humanness and the professional mask.

Being in Denial Hinders Dying

> We know so little about dying. . . . our society does nothing to prepare people for death itself. . . . The nervous little dance that people perform in life is a solitary dance that excludes life's partner, death. When the partner sneaks up and taps us on the shoulder . . . we want to . . . sit out the rest of the dance. But it's too late. Ignorance has robbed us of the final and perhaps richest experience of our lives, that is death. (Perrin, 1988, p. 35)

Many echoes from other cultures and other times tell us that death is a part of life. The Mexican people have historically woven death into their traditions, folk art, family life, and religion. As long ago as A.D. 911 the Swiss monk Notker Balbulus observed that "in the midst of life, we are in death." But North Americans are different: We deny death. Despite our culture's continuing denial of death, gerontology practitioners are acutely aware of, and more frequently confronted with, death than are most other professionals. At the same time we are products of our culture. Because we are afraid of our own dying and the dying of loved ones, we who are helpers avoid countertransference issues as we would the plague.

We often exclude planning for death and dying, and even ignore opportunities provided by the client and the system to include the dying process as an appropriate part of service and treatment. When one hospital staff person was asked to give a new patient a copy of the directive to physicians (including a preference for "no code" and a waiver of extraordinary measures to prolong life), she told the patient, "If you sign it we won't give you any treatment in an emergency; if you don't sign it we'll keep you alive." With those instructions the patient chose treatment—whatever that meant!

A young social worker in one of Kübler-Ross's early death and dying seminars was unusually forthright about her countertransference feelings:

> One of the main reasons why many of us avoid any talk of death is the awful and unbearable feeling that there is nothing we can say or do to comfort the patient. . . . I always felt that old age and sickness was so devastating . . . It seemed to me that the problem of illness and death was so unsolvable and therefore these people could not be helped. (Kübler-Ross, 1975, p. xvi)

This social worker felt helpless when facing illness and aging, partly because she had not begun to face her own fears. Choosing to be helpless is one way of avoiding the reality of one's own disability and dying. Critical to this young woman's feelings of helplessness and hopelessness was her definition of "help." If help meant *cure*, rather than *care*, she was correct to feel devastated: Old age and death cannot be "cured." Dying people make us feel incompetent and unsuccessful when we are wedded to the cure model. But if we subscribe to the care model, and let go of trying to reverse death, we can provide a high quality of care by being with the dying without embarrassment or feelings of inadequacy.

Several years ago I experienced an atmosphere completely opposite to many in which helplessness, denial and control pervade.

There was no sense of embarrassment or incompetence when I visited Mother Teresa's Hospice for men dying of AIDS in New York City. When I asked one sister if the patients preferred being alone in the final stage of dying her response was, "Most of the men like us to be with them. Many of them have been rejected by their families, and have been more alone than they wished. So we take turns, and sit beside them. We just tuck them in and wait."

I cannot imagine a more splendid example of helping the dying than to "tuck them in and wait" with them. It brings images of tucking children in, waiting for them to go to sleep—the little death that occurs each night. It is comforting to them, and to their parents. The staff at Mother Teresa's Hospice have translated that comforting role to the final sleep. I spelled other volunteers by the bedside of Larry, who could no longer speak or move, and chose not to open his eyes. There was a peaceful feeling in his room; tender attention in case he might need anything, but respect for his personal space as he withdrew more and more quietly into himself.

I asked how it was for the staff to live in the midst of dying twenty-four hours a day. One beautiful sister said, "It's hard for us—we get attached to the men, and we miss them. But when they're suffering it's a great relief to see them go." I was profoundly affected by the acceptance of death there: neither a hurrying to get it over, nor a holding on to patients to hinder their leaving. An engaging young patient told me he was freer than he'd ever been in his life. "I was so hard on myself all my life," he said. "Now I have my bird (a parakeet in a cage), my books, and my music. I have everything I need!"

After the first shock of entering the old brownstone house and finding that "in the midst of death, we were in life" (to turn around the saying from Notker Balbulus), I suddenly felt very competent and helpful. I swept floors, dusted, disinfected furniture, made lunch, served breakfast, and sat with Larry who was imminently dying. In this atmosphere pretense and denial, which drain so much of the life energy of dying people and their families, found no home. The men did not pretend to feel good if they didn't, and they didn't look at you or talk to you if they had no energy to do so. But in the pauses between pain there was laughter and truth and reality.

Being Honest Helps the Patient and the Practitioner

Caroline Preston, Professor Emeritus at the University of Washington, had been a gerontologist for 40 and more years. She had looked at aging and mortality from the outside. At 72 she was forced to look at them from the inside. In the last article she ever wrote when she was still "raging against the dying of the light," Preston (1987) said:

> If you are exceedingly fortunate, you will have someone who can look your dyingness straight in the face and share your terror: "How can I not be among you?" Such a confidante must be carefully chosen or you will meet with averted eyes, throat clearing, and eagerly welcome change of subject. (p. 10)

Caroline had experienced well-meaning friends who denied her dying by telling her how terrific she looked, and by avoiding her candid reports of how she was doing with her cancer.

Have you ever noticed the incredibly cheerful competence in acute care wards and oncologists' offices? One of the rules of professionals of all kinds who work with dying people is to be helpful, hopeful, and happy, especially when there are no answers to the patients' questions and when the professionals are feeling profoundly helpless. A dying cancer patient (Siegel, 1986) wrote of her need for honesty:

> Although everyone around me was trying his best to be light-hearted and optimistic, somehow the effect on me was just the opposite. Suddenly being thrust into a situation where everyone behaved only positively while around me made me realize to what extent I was no longer part of that world.
>
> The doctors and nurses who cared for me could not always have a good day. They must have been tired of turning me over in bed or hearing me complain. But, I never saw that. The lab technician taking a blood sample must have been frustrated because my veins were so hard to find. But, she always smiled through gritted teeth. Many times I heard the medical staff outside my door talking in agitated tones. But then, they always appeared in my room as if they were actors going onstage in a well-rehearsed role. (Siegel, 1986, p. 188)

Because some of us have a deep level of discomfort in the face of terminal illness, and because we *do* care about many patients and it hurts us to see their pain, we put on our "professional armor." We justify it by telling ourselves we are making it easier for the dying person. In truth, it protects us, not the dying—or does it? We find ourselves caught in a deception. We wall off the countertransferential inheritance that can bring honest feelings and experiences to our work.

How much a part of her world would this dying patient have felt if the lab technician had said, "It's so frustrating not to find a vein! It must be awful for you to have to go through this again and again with me, and I'm angry at myself because I can't do better for you." Expressing her anger and identifying that she was not mad at the patient might have allowed the technician to laugh with relief rather than smiling through gritted teeth. Let's complicate this story with the possibility that the lab technician had recently had a benign tumor removed, but her fear had not diminished because cancer had taken her grandmother and one sister. The power of recognizing her personal responses to this patient— connected with herself and her family—would have led her to a more congruent and real relationship with the patient. And this need not take much time or much self-disclosure. It is a commitment on the part of helping people to be honest with dying people, instead of creating distance, alienation, and isolation because we feel we have to hide our own personal experiences and fears of dying.

At Mother Teresa's Hospice and in some other settings I am now encountering an uncommonly honest and real atmosphere where people are treated as if they are alive until the moment they die. To create this kind of atmosphere, we professionals must consult our values and biases, our own life developmental stages, our fears, and the unfinished business with dying in our own families. If we do not, we may find ourselves caught in helping behaviors that are meaningless both to us and to our clients. This honesty among professionals needs to be practiced and modeled in in- service training programs. Supervisors, trainers, and consultants need to lead the way by giving permission to staff and volunteers to use their best professional judgment in being honest with pa- tients and clients.

Group consultation is especially effective, because it is hard for us to be honest with ourselves and each other about our imperfections. If the consultant or group leader can create a setting where professionals can say to one another, "Here's where I blew it," we can all learn together how not to "blow it" the next time. I saw this illustrated dramatically in a workshop I gave for professionals who worked with dementia, traumatic brain injury, and suicide. One of the participants was courageous enough to share how difficult it had been for her to try to help suicidal patients at a time when she herself had been contemplating suicide. It gave the others at the seminar permission to confront their own personal connections to the grief, anger, guilt, loss, and depression that their clients were experiencing. As these professionals shared their fears that their strong emotions diminished them as helpers, a deep level of compassion and honesty emerged. Compassion and honesty are, of course, a measure of what is needed to serve not only patients but ourselves as well.

The Paradox:
Being Helpless *Together* Empowers Us Both

When we honestly ask ourselves which persons . . . mean the most to us, we often find that it is those who, instead of giving much advice, solutions, or cures, have chosen rather to share our pain and touch our wounds with a gentle and tender hand. The friend who can . . . stay with us in an hour of grief and bereavement, who can tolerate not-knowing, not-curing, not-healing, and face us with the reality of our powerlessness, that is the friend who cares. (Siegel, 1986, p. x)

Professional helpers normally don't think of themselves as "friends" to their clients and patients; but, in fact, being a professional friend implies limit-setting, a clear understanding between patient and helper, and ethical parameters. It also implies appropriate caring—particularly when there are no medical, psychological, social, or psychiatric solutions. And it necessitates looking at whatever countertransference is occurring. In the simplest terms, it means *being* there for the dying person. It is not by accident that the headings in this chapter are Being Honest, Being Helpless, etc. It is a highly professional and often difficult skill to be fully present with terminally ill people. Our physical presence is a powerful tool, even more so when we are bereft of words and feel we have nothing to give. In his book *The Path of Least Resistance* Robert Fritz (1984) illustrates how important it is for helpers to receive as well as to give.

> Many people with whom I work have a natural desire to serve. In a sense, they are experts at giving. However, they are often inept at receiving. Many who spend much of their lives supporting others have not developed the ability to receive . . . no one is served any better by your inability to receive. If anything, it only teaches the people being served by you how *not* to receive the service you are giving them. (p. 144)

The skill of providing nonverbal support depends on the ability to receive from the dying person. This is a two-way feedback system in which eyes that look past us or into ours, hand movements, the turning of the head, breathing, the color of the skin, and sounds are all important communications. This is a different approach than superimposing clinical and professional opinion based on a previous diagnosis, encapsulated in the following statement: "I've worked with stroke for fifteen years so I know exactly what to expect!" It is hard to allow ourselves to see each new person with fresh eyes after many years. But there is no other way to respect the uniqueness of each dying person than to acknowledge our own helplessness in the face of death, and to receive cues from each patient.

Exploration of countertransferential experiences in our families of birth and in our families of choice is important when we find ourselves feeling impotent in our professional roles. For example, helpers from any kind of dysfunctional family will want to clarify and identify personal "hooks" such as (1) difficulties giving up control to the dying person; (2) investment in "fixing" patients and their families; and (3) echoes that remain of loved ones lost in a similar manner.

My experience as a consultant to hospice staffs has taught me a great deal about their struggle with themselves when patients die "too soon" or "take too long" to die. This means when patients die before the medical indicators prescribe they "should", or when patients linger beyond any understanding according to medical indices. Acknowledging helplessness and frustration helps these excellent hospice professionals (volunteers, home health aides, bereavement counselors, social workers, nurses, chaplains) to reduce their stress. They speak often, in their consultation and support sessions, about their own experiences with fathers, mothers, husbands, and children who have died. And they make connections between the patients they are now serving and their own personal and family experiences. They provide a powerful support for each other, and they achieve this through their honesty and their confrontation of their countertransferential reactions to working full time with the dying.

I want to give one final example of how mutual helplessness paradoxically empowers dying people and their helpers. In this case the empowerment had to do with telling the truth and with the ability to let go. One of the hardest—and most beautiful—experiences I have had, as caregiving friend for my mentor in gerontology as she died of cancer, was watching her oncologist say goodbye to her. When she could no longer walk and could not get to her doctor's office, I phoned him to come to her home. He was one of the last important professionals, and males, in her life. She had not permitted herself to hear him when he told her, several months prior to her death, that he could no longer treat the cancer—only the symptoms. She needed to hear that from him as she did not believe us, her friends and hospice team. At first he said he could not make a home visit. I asked him again; he paused, and said he had not made a home visit before. I reminded him that he was a very important person and doctor to her, and that I suspected she might be a significant patient to him. Then I asked the third time, "Will you come to see her?"

He came, and it was a difficult and profound experience for him. They spoke about hope, pain, and desire to die. He asked her when she wanted to die, and once she understood there was nothing more to be done she cried out, "Yesterday!" They said goodbye, more with looks and pauses than words. When he left her room she smiled at him—something she'd not done for days—and her eyes followed him out the door as far as they could. I believe the closure was as important to him as to her. Such closure is seldom accomplished without at least a look at the personal-professional connection, and the depth of loss felt by the professional helper.

I do not know if the oncologist had lost family members to cancer, or why he chose this field. I do know that he put himself on the line when he dared to visit a dying patient in her home—not to treat her or cure her, but to face his own and her helplessness in the face of death. I also know that it enabled my friend to let go, for she began doing her inner work from that moment on and died a few days later. She badly needed the truth from him one more time, for she had been denying her death and was in much physical, mental, and emotional pain because of it.

Being Professional Is Being Human

We live in a society in which control of emotions and the display of "proper behavior" are highly rewarded. We also live in a society in which joining a profession is associated with something called "professional behavior." . . . The grieving patient . . . not only makes us feel guilty, but he also makes us feel scared about our own ability to sustain a relationship without losing the mask identified with a professional stance. In interviews with physicians and nurses, the fear of crying . . . is tragically a block to the display of some of the genuine concern which is present among many who, in their own frustration, have felt conflict between their concern and the mask they felt they must wear. (Kübler-Ross, 1975, pp. 11-12)

Professional perfectionism is an occupational hazard for practitioners. Countless helpers who work with the dying refuse to admit to themselves that they are in an ongoing state of bereavement. Yet, not to know what our bodies and emotions tell us is a deeply fragmenting stressor to the mind and the whole human system, and our professional behaviors suffer when we collude in this kind of self-deception. I offer myself as an example of a divided and conflicted helper.

I shall call him Harry. I had worked with him, and with his family, a long time. He suffered from an untreatable dementia, and as the years rolled by he just curled up emotionally, then mentally, and finally physically. When he died the family asked if I would help lead the memorial service since I knew him during his final life transition. I said I'd be happy to, and I meant it—never dreaming I had not kept up with my grieving along the way. I usually have no difficulty speaking, and my role was not heavy as the service was planned to be participative, but somehow I was stuck. The morning of the service came, and I couldn't even sit down and write an outline. By early afternoon I was in a minor panic. I did not want to go, and yet I loved Harry, his wife, and his family.

Two colleagues who knew me well stopped by my office, took one look at my face, and knew something was wrong. Instead of giving me advice, or verbally questioning me, they enfolded me in their arms and hugged me. I began to sob. "I'm going to miss him! I haven't even begun to let go of him." I began remembering: The time in my office when he grieved for the loss of himself, the tears sliding down his cheeks; the time I visited his adult day center in fear that he wouldn't recognize me, but he smiled and we both knew that I was someone familiar to him; the sadness the last time he recognized he was on the edge of not remembering anything any more; and the time his family and I kept vigil by his nursing home bed when his body was present but he seemed a million miles away.

My two colleagues held me for awhile, and I caught up with my grief a little until I was able to drive to the church and be present with Harry's family. We all grieved together, and I was more on balance again. Only later did I let myself know that my own mother was failing, and that I had had professional expectations of myself to help Harry and his family more than I'd been able to. This is so often the way with us helpers: We try extra hard to help clients and patients when we can't help our own family members. My mother had, by this time, had one diagnosis of Alzheimer's disease. I did not agree with the diagnosis, but this did not erase the fear that my mother would become like Harry. At the moment my colleagues came in, I was in a state of bereavement, but pretending to myself that I was not. Harry was, and always will be, an important person to me. He taught me how to let go of one part of the whole person—the loss of mind—with grief and with honesty. He was worth grieving over. This is human, and part of being professional is being human.

When my mother was deteriorating inch by inch in a nursing home, and I was in and out of awareness that my friend's cancer was growing, I needed to be unusually aware of any clients and families who might have stimulated countertransference in me. These connections are critical to recognize: (1) the possibility of transferring or terminating clients for whom *we* are inappropriate;

(2) the possibility of taking sick leave or time off work to center ourselves, heal, and get back on balance; (3) the probability of getting therapy, or being in a professional or any other kind of support group, in order to get through the heavy bereavement stage; and (4) the necessity of relying on good supervision and consultation for insights about clients and our countertransference reactions.

I increasingly recommend that helpers of all kinds start professional support groups where countertransference can be looked at as a positive therapeutic process and the basis for growth and understanding. Grieving is one professional behavior we resist when we subscribe to the myth that we must be strong and helpful at all times. We need to shift to the belief that grieving for the cumulative losses that occur as a natural part of our work is necessary. The fine art of letting go of clients and patients depends on the confrontation of countertransference issues and doing effective grief work ourselves.

Summary

We who are helping professionals experience all the awe, mystery, fear, and denial regarding death as do all other human beings. We need to be aware of, and behaviorally responsible for, our countertransference reactions and responses. Denial of our feelings toward dying people is often a disservice to them and may be crippling to us. Being honest with the dying brings us closer to them and allows us to be more effective. Acknowledging helplessness in the face of death is often therapeutic for both the helper and the person being helped. It creates bonding, a team approach to death, and closure. Sharing our humanness in the dying process with clients and with other professionals keeps us in balance, authentic to ourselves, and congruent to our patients and clients. Grieving appropriately provides self-care and deepens our ability to continue work with dying people in creative and supportive ways.

All the blood children and the took-ins, like me, came home from Minneapolis and Chicago, where they had relocated years ago. . . . They were struck down with grief and bereavement to be sure, every one of them. . . . From the back (of the funeral) we watched all the children and the mourners as they hunched over their prayers, their hands stuffed full of Kleenex. It was someplace in that long sad service that my vision shifted. I began to see things different, more clear. The family kneeling down turned to rocks in a field. It struck me how strong and reliable grief was, and death. Until the end of time, death would be our rock.

So I had perspective on it all, for death gives you that. (Erdrich, 1984, pp. 210-211)

References

Erdrich, L. (1984). *Love medicine* (pp. 210-211). New York: Holt, Rinehart & Winston.

Fritz, R. (1984). *The path of least resistance*. Salem, MA: DMA, Inc.

Gino, C. (1982). *The nurse's story*. New York: Simon & Schuster.

Kübler-Ross, E. (1975). *Death The final stage of growth*. Englewood Cliffs, NJ: Prentice-Hall.

Perrin, S. (1988). *Leah*. London: Wisdom Publications.

Preston, C. (1987, August 10). *The aging connection* San Francisco: American Society on Aging.

Siegel, B. (1986). *Love, medicine & miracles*. New York: Harper & Row.

Watt, R. (1988, October/November). *Family Services Newsletter*. Seattle, WA: Family Services.

3

Effective Intervention and Negative Emotional Reactions to Suicidal Elders

Fifty percent of people over 65 who kill themselves see a health care professional in the month preceding their death. Counter-transference feelings in helping professionals may be a factor in the high suicide rate among the elderly; becoming aware of these feelings can be important in preventing suicide. Health care professionals often seem less interested in elder suicide than in teen suicide, and some do not see the former as much of a problem. However, suicide is on the minds of thousands of older men and women whom we see as family, friends, neighbors, clients, and patients.

While older people represent approximately 11% of the population, they account for 25% of all reported suicides (Blazer, Bachar, & Manton, 1986). Minimum estimates range from 6,000 to 10,000 elder suicides in the United States annually. Many older suicides are not reported as such. Since many of these suicides are committed by isolated, lonely, older people, there may be no friends or family who care about the cause of death. Or the friends or family may be too afraid to ask. Additionally, suicides are often mistaken as natural death, especially in cases of overdosing, because many older people take a variety of medications. When the taboo surrounding suicide is considered, inaccurate labeling of death is not surprising.

The peak suicide rate occurs in men in their eighties. White males over 75 have a higher rate of suicide than any other age group. However, suicide is not an option reserved for white males. Studies have indicated an increase in suicides of nonwhite men over the past 10 years (Manton, Blazer, & Woodbury, 1987).

For the population as a whole, there are approximately 10 to 20 attempts for every completed suicide. Ratios for the young are as high as 200 attempts for one completed suicide. For older people the ratio of attempts to suicide completions narrows dramatically to 4:1. Thus, an older person who contemplates suicide is more likely to complete the act. There are several reasons for this. First, older people employ lethal methods when attempting suicide; second, older people experience greater social isolation; and finally, older people generally have poor powers of recuperation, which make them less likely to recover from a suicidal act.

Focus on the Need, Not the Act

Currently in the Western world, suicide is a conscious act of self-induced annihilation, best understood as a multidimensional malaise in a needful individual who defines an issue for which the suicide is perceived as the best solution. (Shneidman, 1985)

This definition is important because it tells us something about the actor, not only the act of suicide. To focus only on the self-destructive act perpetuates our fears of the suicidal older person. As a public health nurse once remarked, "When an older patient refers to suicidal feelings, I try to ignore them because I feel scared." This helper fears the destructive act of suicide, forgetting the needful state of the older person. If the helper ignores the feelings, a suicidal older person may not receive the necessary help and a tragedy may result. For example, an older woman explained to me that she refused to tell her doctor about her thoughts of suicide because "she (the doctor) will have me hospitalized if I tell her that sometimes I wish I were dead."

When an older person feels helpless, he or she may decide to choose suicide as a way of dealing with a difficult situation. If they perceive helplessness or denial in their health care professionals, then at-risk elders may think that they have no alternatives other than suicide. By blocking a discussion of suicide, the helper misses an opportunity to connect in a significant way with the older person. Helpers who interact with vulnerable older people must be aware of the feelings they bring into the relationship. Without professionals exercising self-awareness, suicidal cues may be missed or ignored thereby increasing a feeling of helplessness in the needful older person.

The Five Defense Postures

During the 15 years I have worked with suicidal individuals, I have experienced a range of emotional responses to their emergencies. I have had feelings of denial, anger, frustration, sadness, helplessness, fear, irritation, repugnance, and even disgust when confronted by a suicidal person. Conversely, I also have felt compassion, empathy, hope, and love for people in pain. Sometimes the positive feelings are slow to emerge. I have often wondered what prevents those good feelings from spontaneously happening when working with vulnerable older people. According to Maltsberger and Buie (1974) five defense postures inhibit our full awareness of countertransference feelings: repression, distortion, projection, conversion, and reaction formation. These defense postures are useful ways to examine the complex feelings that arise when we face suicidal older people. Many of these are feelings we would prefer not to have.

REPRESSION

Al, age 74, described some of his feelings and the responses of his doctor:

When it comes to being crippled or incapacitated that's the end for me because I have no intentions whatsoever of being in a nursing home or having anyone push me around in a wheel chair. I've been going to a doctor. He is supposed to be a specialist in geriatrics. He said there's nothing the matter with me that either getting married or taking a cruise wouldn't cure. I don't think he knows much about old people's problems. I'm not wanting to go back. When anyone tells me that getting married or taking a cruise will solve my problems . . . I could take a cruise and jump overboard. That would solve it. I could get married and show my wife how to use my pistol. That would solve it.

Al has been widowed for several years. He lives alone in a residential section of an urban neighborhood. He uses alcohol daily. He is unwilling to go to a senior center or engage in group activities. Having worked in a variety of jobs throughout his adult life (including a position in a nursing home), he is very concerned about remaining independent; he fears institutionalization.

Al's fears of abandonment and dependence triggered a counter-transference reaction in the doctor: denial. Through repression, denial is veiled. By not directly confronting Al's suicidal thought ("that's the end for me"), the doctor lost Al's trust. Instead of seeing an older person who is desperately afraid of abandonment and dependent living, the doctor chose to see an older man who is "healthy," exaggerating symptoms, and simply complaining about being lonely. By saying that there was nothing the matter with Al that getting married or going on a cruise would not cure, the doctor distanced himself from Al and trivialized Al's problem. In a sense, Al's fears are actually being enacted by the doctor. Al felt misunderstood and abandoned and chose not to return to this doctor. For Al, and those like him, another potential source of support has been eliminated. By repressing his counter-transference feeling of denial, this doctor did not effectively assess Al's suicidal feelings and, in fact, exacerbated his sense of abandonment.

Instead of avoiding and denying Al's fear, this doctor had other choices. He could have allowed Al to discuss his feelings. Yet, this does take time and it may be frightening. However, the time is well justified when speaking to an older adult who feels suicidal. Elders who talk about suicide are the ones who attempt it. The doctor could have asked Al about a suicide plan. Since Al had a gun, he would be at a high risk for suicide. The doctor and Al would agree that the gun be removed from his apartment. For example, during the time that the doctor and Al will work together, the gun could be placed in a safety deposit box. The content of their subsequent meetings could address Al's fears, focusing special attention on his feelings of suicide. Once the risk of suicide has decreased, the doctor can go about the task he is trained to do: help. Initially, he can help by creating a safe environment where Al can discuss his feelings. When Al senses that his suicidal thoughts do not threaten his professional caregiver, an important bond is forged. No longer needing to defend his suicidal thoughts, Al can look at other alternatives.

When did the doctor repress the denial? This defensive posture probably arose when Al spoke about ending his life. Al's loneliness and destructive feelings may have overwhelmed the doctor. He may have thought: "How can I help this man when I have so many people to see?" "I'm going through a divorce myself. I'm lonely too. We're all alone. There's nothing I can do," or "I simply don't have the time to deal with this. Why doesn't he just pull himself together?" By being self-aware, the doctor could try another approach, one that would not alienate Al. Once he established suicidal intent, the doctor could say, "I'm wondering if you could tell me more about your feelings," or "I really want to help you work through these fears." Or, if he won't listen to Al's feelings, the doctor could refer Al to someone who would. The doctor intuitively knows that Al needs help. However, there are no easy answers. The alternatives will take time to explore. When the doctor acknowledges his own feelings of denial, he may recognize that he typically feels this way when confronted by an older person who may be at risk of suicide. Thus, rather than succumbing to denial, this countertransference reaction can be used as another tool in evaluating potential risk of suicide in older patients. It would be important for this professional to look at suicides and old people in his own family.

Unlike other age populations, where the helping professional is one of many others in a person's life, the gerontology professional may be the only person in a position to help in the life of an isolated, at-risk older person. Al's doctor may have had countertransference feelings of malice, aversion, or repugnance. These negative feelings may be difficult for us to acknowledge in ourselves. Yet, malice toward the suicidal older person may manifest itself through thoughts such as "Why am I wasting time on this person when I have more important matters that require my attention?" or "He's just going to die anyway. He's old. I wish he would stop talking and go home." By repressing these aversive feelings, the doctor may not have been paying attention to what Al was saying.

How do we know when we are repressing negative feelings? Everyone's route toward self-awareness will probably take a different path. However, aversive feelings are often expressed through drowsiness, boredom, anxiety, or restlessness. Aversive feelings may also be expressed through yawning, too frequent glances at the clock, or other signs of inattention that convey the feeling "I do not want to be with you." By repressing his own negative feelings, the doctor was unable to ascertain what Al was doing to arouse his hostility. Al is a frightened, lonely older man who is contemplating taking his own life. The doctor could examine his negative feelings by asking, "I'm feeling annoyed and tired. Why is this? I wasn't feeling this way before Al entered my office. My feelings must be related to something going on between us. I'd better pay close attention to what Al is saying." This is one way to examine our countertransference and use it as a springboard back to the problems of the vulnerable older person.

DISTORTION

John, 75, is divorced and alone. He abuses alcohol and has been drinking heavily for several years. He made one prior suicide attempt approximately 10 years ago when he was divorced. He is discussing his second suicide attempt, which occurred recently.

I thought if I took enough pills, that would finish me off, along with the booze and everything. I couldn't even get out of bed. So I called an ambulance and they took me out on a stretcher. I don't remember if anyone asked me if I tried to kill myself. They pushed me out of the hospital at 3:30 a.m. I would never think of going back there. What I want to do is die. I thought if I drank enough booze I'd die but I don't.

The defensive posture illustrated in this example is distortion. The countertransference feelings that are not being identified by the hospital staff include hopelessness, indifference, pity, and anger. The hospital team—intake worker, psychiatric resident, and nurse—perceive John as a hopeless case. This may be due to the observation that John is an older alcoholic who is dirty, drunk, and desperate. Not wanting to admit to hopelessness, the hospital team members ignore their countertransference reactions, and John's desperate plight as well. Rather than perceiving John as a man who feels incredibly hopeless, alone, and suicidal, these professional helpers distort the scenario to reflect a person who is misusing vital city services. Since their own feelings of hopelessness are strong, the hospital team does very little to reassure John because they believe that nothing they do will help. Out of the hopelessness evolve feelings of indifference, pity, and anger. Because it is difficult to be in a helping role with feelings such as these, it is easy to understand the next step, which is premature discharge from the protective hospital environment. When John is removed from their care and their sight, their feelings of hopelessness subside. Unfortunately, John feels rejected, just as he did when he was divorced. His suicidal feelings escalate. He returns to his destructive thoughts, seeing suicide as a release from unendurable psychological pain.

If the hospital team was trained to look at their own countertransference feelings (or instructed on how to recognize countertransference and defensive postures), they might have responded differently to John. Distortion takes place when *we view John as a hopeless case*, rather than understanding that *John feels hopeless*. Feelings of hopelessness are common for suicidal people. John's hopelessness results from being in a bad situation with neither goals to look forward to nor means of improving his condition. Although John lacks the emotional resources to change his situation, he is likely to respond positively to anyone who conveys hope. Rather than immediate discharge, a strategy directed toward teaching John some helping skills is warranted. John's dependency on alcohol is certainly a major problem. However, it is important not to become overwhelmed. Something can be done. As an older volunteer in our Geriatric Outreach Program once remarked, "Working with suicidal people has taught me the luxury of being inconvenienced." The going is slow in a case like John's because he has been coping negatively for a long time. It is easy to slide into identifying with John's hopelessness and giving up. Being aware of these countertransference feelings may help remind us that although the process may be slow, it is not hopeless.

PROJECTION

Jane, a 62-year-old married woman has had a history of mental illness and a myriad of physical problems including obesity, heart problems, and arthritis. Since her husband is active in the community, Jane spends a great deal of time alone.

Frightened by being alone, Jane telephones a suicide prevention center for support. She makes repeated calls on one occasion. After several hours, the trained volunteers who have spoken with her concur that Jane should not call anymore, although they rate her suicide risk as high. The volunteers are very angry, agitated, and resistant to the help offered by their supervisor. When the supervisor encourages them to set limits and proposes alternatives such as hospitalization, or identifying one volunteer in the group to work with her, the volunteers are hostile.

In this case, the volunteers used projection to avoid their countertransference feelings. Although they rated Jane as a high suicide risk, they also dreaded and feared her actually carrying out the act. Their underlying assumption was: Jane is going to kill herself no matter what we do or say. These volunteers felt as helpless to positively intervene as Jane felt helpless to go on living. The difficulty here is that the volunteers were taking Jane's suicidal threats and her seeming unwillingness to be helped personally. Despite their well-intentioned suggestions, Jane continued to despair. Rather than evaluating the effectiveness of their suggestions, they projected their hostility onto Jane and onto their supervisor. Jane's level of risk for suicide was lost amidst the clutter of emotion that was going on. Projection is identified by the following statements of the volunteers:

We feel upset with Jane.

We feel angry at Jane.

We can't set limits with her.

She won't consider any alternatives.

She's not helpable.

We feel like telling Jane not to call anymore.

What they did not say, but may have thought, is that "Jane should kill herself because she is a miserable person who is making us feel miserable too." A person worthy of their help would have accepted their suggestions and stopped calling. Jane's inability to respond positively to their help stretched their helping skills beyond a tolerable point.

Projecting negative feelings onto the suicidal person is a way of freeing ourselves of these "bad" or hostile feelings. Projecting onto our supervisors accomplishes the same purpose!

Training that guides helpers into an understanding of negative countertransference and projection will give them the clues they need to respond to situations like Jane's. Had these helpers recognized their own angry and helpless feelings, they could have understood that Jane was feeling angry and helpless, too. By projecting these feelings onto Jane, they increased Jane's already agitated state, which resulted in additional phone calls.

CONVERSION

Another way of avoiding uncomfortable countertransference feelings is by conversion. When negative feelings are triggered in an interaction, for example, the feelings are turned inward against the self. For instance, helping professionals may have fantasies that they would commit suicide if they were in the same situation as the vulnerable elder. Thus, the helper senses strong feelings and converts or transforms them into an internal process. Rather than asking older clients about their suicidal feelings, the helper may begin to dwell on his or her own fears.

Mary, a 78-year-old widow, is confined to her bed, depressed, and thinking of killing herself. Her room is small and stuffy. The windows do not open. I have accompanied a graduate

student in counseling to assess Mary's suicide risk. During
the visit, the intern is silent. Upon leaving the apartment, she
quickly departs; I hear from her the next day. She tells me that
she could become like this older woman in 30 years. She
would kill herself before she would become so isolated. Carefully, I encourage the intern to express her feelings. She says
"I hate her. I hate her apartment. I can't stand myself for
hating her."

This intern had intense feelings that were stimulated during the
visit. With some prodding, she was able to express the negative
countertransference feeling she experienced: hate. This feeling of
hate was incongruent with this mental health worker's task,
which was to alleviate suffering. Thus, the direction of the countertransference feeling of hate was converted from the older person ("I hate her") to the self ("I can't stand myself for hating her.").
With exploration, the intern discovered that she felt inadequate in
addressing issues related to suicide risk, and that she was fearful
of her own old age and aloneness, as well as her personal suicidal
ideation. The combined effect of the depressed older person and
the stifling environment wreaked havoc with her feelings.

Through a process of acknowledging her own feelings, this
intern was able to use her negative countertransference feeling of
hate as an assessment tool. She believed that this woman wanted
to kill herself. She hated her, however, for creating a situation
whereby the intern had to test her skills. Rather than risking
dealing with the older person's despair, she turned the hate inward. Thus, she could avoid the potential suicidal situation of the
client by dealing only with her own internal feelings. After our
discussion, however, this intern could use the countertransference
feeling of hate to alert herself to a serious situation. She and I
agreed that she needed to have additional training and practice in
working with suicidal older people in order to lessen her feelings
of inadequacy, hate, and fear.

REACTION FORMATION

Countertransference feelings of inadequacy can manifest themselves in the reverse as rescue fantasies. The helper, in this case,
feeling panicked, meddles in the older person's affairs. The helper

experiences great urgency and may not evaluate the risk of suicide appropriately, by misreading cues and interpreting every action as suicidal. The older person may then agree that the helper is responsible for his or her life and be all too willing to submit to helplessness and dependency.

Anna, an 80-year-old resident of a senior housing unit, was grieving over the death of her long-term companion. Although she had some physical limitations, she was capable of living alone and managing her life. A failed suicide attempt in her bereavement brought her to our attention. Support was offered by a 40-year-old female graduate student in psychology.

It was agreed that a weekly visit and telephone reassurance calls were in order. The intern was asked to do the weekly visit. In a few weeks this intern had increased the visiting to twice a week. She also initiated her own calls. Soon frantic calls were received by her supervisor at late hours regarding Anna's suicide potential. To requests from the supervisor to limit involvement, the intern refused. She felt strongly that she was the only one who understood Anna.

This intern was unable to step back and reflect on her countertransference responses. It was only when she was relieved of working with Anna, and intensified her supervision, that she could express feelings of inadequacy. Because she did not trust her assessment skills, she worried about Anna, losing a great deal of sleep in the process. This intern was so immersed in anxiety and rescue fantasies that she was unable to help this elder, or to differentiate between bereavement and suicidal ideation. In choosing to "rescue" Anna, she limited Anna's ability to cope in healthy ways. Anna wanted attention desperately. Because her helper was anxious, Anna manipulated her easily. Unfortunately, Anna may have acted out suicidal behavior to insure the intern's constant attention. Because the intern's assessment skills were weakened due to the anxiety, a potentially serious situation might have been overlooked simply because of the helper's sheer exhaustion.

Countertransference and the Survivors

Suicide does not end with the person who died. Family members, friends, neighbors, and helping professionals can all be affected and "infected." Countertransference plays a part here, if the helping professional feels apathy or exhibits a premature need to close down discussion of suicide. This can be recognized when a helper tells a middle-aged woman whose father took his own life to, "Look at it this way. Your father is out of pain. He lived a long, good life. It is time for you to get on with your life." Another helping professional tells a resident of a senior housing unit where another tenant leaped to his death from a seventh story window, "Forget about him. He would have killed himself anyway. There wasn't anything we could have done to save him."

These helpers could benefit from an examination of their countertransference feelings of apathy and avoidance. By expressing a lack of interest in the death, the helpers once again are conveying hopelessness. The grievers, therefore, may feel unable or reluctant to share their own feelings related to the death because they, too, feel hopeless.

Countertransference feelings of apathy and avoidance may be a protection from fears the helper has of sudden death, losses, or aging. Learning to recognize these feelings would enable the helper to encourage opportunities for grief work rather than avoidance. It is especially important, when working with survivors, to look at one's suicide and grief connections to one's own family members. As helpers, we must listen to the voices of the grievers who strongly question the role of the helpers in their relationship with their loved ones prior to their death. The implication for examining countertransference feelings by all helpers is explicit in the following case of a middle-aged griever.

While her mother was asleep, her father went into another room in the family home and shot himself through the head. He was 69 years old. He had said that he was afraid that he may have had to use a wheelchair soon. His eyes were failing. He spoke about the possibility of moving into a retirement community. For many years he frequently consulted with a variety of doctors regarding his failing physical health.

Since my father had many health problems throughout his life, I wish a doctor would have intervened. Now I would recommend to my father's doctors that they ask him about his feelings. Maybe he was mad at my mother and wanted to murder her. Instead, he killed himself. It seems like someone should have asked him about these feelings. I wish someone would have asked him if he were thinking about killing himself. There is no telling what change may have taken place had someone inquired. If we would have known, maybe I would not have experienced such a shock.

Rational Suicide?

What about the possibility that suicide is appropriate in some cases? Rational suicides do happen, but people take a lot of time to consider them and do careful planning, usually in consultation with someone from the medical world. If a helping professional thinks, "If I were this person, I would kill myself," it is important for the professional to examine these feelings. Are they coming from the professional's personal agenda? Or are they truly a response to the needs that the client has expressed? Often, positive feelings about suicide stem from one of the countertransference defense postures discussed above. Although I have discussed only negative countertransference emotions, accurate empathy and positive interventions result from awareness of *all* of the professional helper's feelings and personal-professional connections.

Summary

Elderly suicide is an enormous social problem that is not simply going to disappear. One way to prevent older individuals from killing themselves is to be alert to our countertransference feelings. As helpers, we must recognize feelings that we have been trained not to have. Unpopular and uncomfortable feelings can be discussed through supervision sessions, professional support groups, consultation, conferences, inservice training, and many other methods.

Suicidal older people do not always express their feelings directly. Rather than defend ourselves against the very real emotions that surface within us as helpers, an understanding and acceptance of the denial, aversion, hopelessness, anger, anxiety, and other negative feelings may be the only information we have that tells us that the situation is life threatening. An awareness of our "gut" feelings may be the only barometer we have to accurately assess the level of despair of the vulnerable elder with whom we are interacting. We must learn to hear the silent despair of many of our older community members. It really comes down to listening—to ourselves and to the elder with whom we are working.

References

Blazer, D. G., Bachar, J. R., & Manton, K. G. (1986). Suicide in late life: Review and commentary. *JAGS, 34*(7), 519-525.
Maltsberger, J. T., & Buie, D. H. (1974). Countertransference hate in the treatment of suicidal patients. *Archives of General Psychiatry, 30,* 625-633.
Manton, K. G., Blazer, D. G., & Woodbury, M. A. (1987). Suicide in middle age and later life: Sex and race specific table and cohort analyses. *Journal of Gerontology, 42*(2), 219-227.
Shneidman, E. (1985). *Definition of suicide.* New York: John Wiley.

4

A Mirror to Our Souls: Working with Older Adults with AIDS and HIV Illness

MAUREEN O'NEIL

At first glance, aging and AIDS may seem to be very dissimilar experiences. However, many of us who work with people with AIDS have often compared AIDS to an accelerated aging process. As with the aging process, the physical, psychological, and social dimensions of AIDS are multiple. The dynamics of fear, isolation, and stigmatization apply equally to AIDS and aging. The older adult with HIV illness frequently experiences the twofold impact of these negative social responses. It is important for those of us in the helping professions to examine how these negative social responses enter into our roles as helpers. Both ageism and AIDS phobia are driven by the forces of stereotyping, fear, and stigmatization. The person who is HIV infected is feared and shunned. He or she is seen as having perverse morals, being sexually promiscuous, or, worse yet, being a junkie.

Older adults generally are less respected than their younger counterparts. They are seen as having less to contribute to society than younger people. Both the older adult and the person with HIV illness are viewed as drains on our social service and health care delivery systems. Older people are often seen as not needing intimacy, affection, love, or sex. The older gay man or lesbian is frequently seen as maladapted—even more so than their younger gay or lesbian counterparts. Helping professionals often minimize the diversity of ethnicity, class, values, political participation, and sexual orientation among older adults. By doing so, we keep the experience of older adults at a safe emotional distance from ourselves. We circumscribe our role as helper by our view of who older adults are, and ought to be, rather than seeing them as they truly are.

An older adult with HIV illness challenges our stereotypes not only about older adults, but also about people with AIDS. The number of older people who are infected or sick or who have died is growing (Catania, Turner, Kegles, Stall, Pollack, & Coates, 1989). Older people are also partners, lovers, and spouses of those who are ill or who have died. They are parents, grandparents, aunts, uncles, and siblings. Many older adults worry about contracting the HIV virus through sexual contact or blood transfusions.

Fear of contagion probably remains the foremost concern among care providers of people with HIV illness. This is particularly true in health care settings where the risk of blood-to-blood contact is the highest. Many helping professionals now are involved in areas where they feel inexperienced or insecure. For example, in providing health education, practitioners are now asked to take sexual and substance abuse histories as well as to provide safer sex education. Many care providers are now working with client populations that they have not previously encountered.

Care of the patient or client with HIV illness is complex and often emotionally charged, so it is important for each of us to conduct a personal inventory of what is difficult, painful, and challenging as we work in the midst of the largest epidemic of our time. The following sections of this chapter will examine how manifestations of ageism, AIDS phobia, homophobia and the fear of illness, decline, and death often block our capacities to be effective helpers.

Blocks to Effective Helping

One way to recognize countertransference is to acknowledge that it occurs more often than we consciously realize. In fact, it occurs in every human interaction. Usually, it does not prevent us from being able to help people. There are times, however, when we do not hear what our clients are telling us because we are preoccupied with what we are feeling in response to the situation the client is bringing to our attention. Another way to recognize countertransference is to take a good look at some of the assumptions, attitudes and expectations that we bring to the helping situation.

AGEISM

In the case of the older adult with HIV illness, we need to ask ourselves, "What are our expectations about psychological adjustment and behavior in later life?"

Because illness and death are normative life experiences, we often get caught in the trap of minimizing their psychological impact on an older adult. We expect the older adult to cope "maturely" and "appropriately" at this time. This expectation leaves little room for individual differences in coping styles, psychological functioning, or levels of social support available to older adults. We are often unconsciously saying: "It is okay to die if you are old, but not if you are young." This really means: "Your situation matters little because, after all, you are older and you are expected to know how to cope with these things." We minimize the significance of illness and loss in later life. Geriatric medicine has come a long way in the development of a psychosocial approach to the care needs of an older adult. But its development is far from universal in practice. How many times have we heard the physical complaints of older adults being written off as "old age"? Many physicians who treat older adults have little or no experience in the treatment of HIV illness. Consequently, the older adult may need special support and advocacy in getting appropriate sources of medical care.

CONSPIRACY OF SILENCE

Conspiracy of silence is a term that describes the breakdown of communication that develops around someone who has a life-threatening or terminal illness. People around the sick person don't know what to say or do, so they say nothing. They may occupy a great deal of time by talking about everything else except the painfully obvious: "You are dying and I don't know what to say or do." In the case of a person with HIV illness, the situation intensifies, because the patient and often those around him or her feel the stigma of the disease. Consequently, communication can shut down altogether. Everyone is left feeling very isolated and burdened with "the secret." An extreme example of conspiracy of silence is the impulse to withhold the HIV diagnosis from the patient. Rationalizations for this type of thinking are many: "After all, why does he or she really need to know that it is AIDS? What difference will it make in the long run? If he or she finds out that it is AIDS, he or she will only feel stigmatized, alone, and depressed. What good will *that* do?"

As helping professionals, we often mirror the cues and behaviors of the patient, his or her support system, and other care providers. We may try to rationalize our behaviors. We may "assess" that the patient really does not want to know the diagnosis. We may assume that not everyone has the same need for information. We are really saying: "This is much too painful for us to discuss." As a result, we avoid it for the "good" of the patient. By doing this, we may in fact withhold very important information about HIV transmission and infection control as they relate to the sexual activity and needs of the patient. Care providers in medical roles are caught in a trap once the patient begins to ask questions about the illness. The patient's discovery of the lie will come at some point in the course of his or her care, usually when the health care provider can find no way around the truth, or when a new care provider enters the scene.

DESEXUALIZATION

We often assume that older adults are not interested in safer sex education. This assumption clearly comes from the myth that older adults are not sexually active or interested in their own sexuality (see Chapter 12). Therefore, we assume that HIV education and information about risk reduction is of no interest to them. Many helping professionals feel helpless and embarrassed in addressing sexuality issues with older adults. This is particularly true if the older adult does not seem to be asking for such information (Catania et al., 1989).

CONFIDENTIALITY

There is still a high degree of sensationalism surrounding the HIV epidemic. Fear of contagion continues to remain quite high among those in helping roles. Usual practices of confidentiality are likely to break down, as anxiety and the helper's need to talk about it lead to the inadvertent disclosure of patient identity.

The Helper's Response to Specific Groups

Let us now look at some examples in which the older adult is wrestling with an HIV diagnosis. Or, perhaps he or she is the parent, spouse, or partner of someone who is ill. How do certain countertransference issues and dynamics interfere in the helping process?

OLDER GAY MEN

Older gay and bisexual men make up the largest percentage of people over 50 who have HIV illness (Catania et al., 1989). There is a great diversity among older gay people, just as there is among older people in general. Many older gay men and lesbians remember what life was like before the gay liberation movement of the late 1960-70s. They clearly remember the social climate of the 1940s, 1950s, and early 1960s, when they risked being arrested if they were found to be gay or lesbian. Many were arrested or knew friends who were arrested. Many lost their jobs. Because of these experiences, many older gay men and lesbians have chosen not to reveal their sexual orientation for fear of reprisal. The HIV epidemic has awakened their anxiety about disclosure. In fact, by coming out through an HIV diagnosis, the older gay man may have more to risk than his younger counterpart. A lifetime has been built on carefully protecting his sexual orientation. Earlier memories and experiences of anti-gay discrimination and violence are likely to resurface, leaving the older person even more vulnerable at an already vulnerable time.

Jim and Tom have been partners for twenty-three years. They have led a quiet life, and enjoyed the company of a few very close friends. They both have managed to keep their work lives and personal lives very separate. Jim is now ill with AIDS.

Because Jim is unable to get back and forth to the doctor's on his own, Tom now takes him. This is the first time that the office nurse has met Tom. She is shocked to discover that Jim has a partner. She begins to ask them questions about their relationship and how long they have been together. She asks Jim why he hadn't told her sooner that he had a partner. Both Jim and Tom feel very uncomfortable with all of her questions but try to be polite. Finally she asks whether they have settled their legal affairs. In frustration Jim and Tom tell her that this is none of her business. They tell her not to ask them any more questions.

Helper Response: Homophobia

Each of us has a sense of what a family is or ought to be—based largely on our experiences in our families of origin. These experiences significantly influence our views of the world. They are often challenged when we encounter situations that do not fit our world view.

In this example, the office nurse was uncomfortable with Jim and Tom's relationship so she tried to force a discussion with Jim and Tom *about* their relationship. They felt overwhelmed by all of her questions and pushed into a corner; they tried to stop any further questioning. The office nurse tried too hard. In turn, she felt that Jim and Tom were uncooperative. The net result was that all felt angry, and communication broke down. Another health care provider may have sensed Jim and Tom's need for privacy and reluctance to talk about themselves. Yet it would be possible to get to some of the key concerns and worries without forcing a discussion about their relationship. With a couple as private as Jim and Tom, it takes time to figure out the balance between pushing them beyond their limits and addressing key issues that relate to health care.

TRANSFUSION RECIPIENTS

Because more older people are hospitalized for illness and surgery, the likelihood of an older adult having received a blood transfusion during the time blood was not properly screened for the HIV virus is higher than for younger people. Transfusion recipients comprise the second largest group of people age 50 and over who have been diagnosed with AIDS (Catania et al., 1989). Transfusion recipients may also belong to other high risk groups such as gay or bisexual males. People who have contracted HIV illness from transfusions experience a very strong sense of isolation and stigmatization. They may go to great lengths to hide their illness. They frequently feel unable to disclose their diagnosis to anyone, even their closest family members. They are fearful of being associated with anyone else with AIDS. It is often difficult to persuade them to use services for people with HIV illness, thus specialized services have been developed in some regions of the country to meet their psychosocial needs. However, it is often very difficult for a transfusion recipient with HIV infection to utilize a support group. They are often too immobilized and fearful of identification.

Helper Response: Forcing Disclosure

Transfusion recipients often implore care providers to honor the secret of their illness. Sometimes this dilemma can block the helping professional from seeking useful community services that would make the patient's life a little easier. If the professional is not aware of the countertransference hook, he or she can feel backed into a corner, frustrated, and be unable to find ways to be supportive to the patient. The helping professional may focus his or her energy on the belief that life would be better for the patient if he or she would "just tell" family and loved ones. This leaves little, if any, room for the patient to find his or her own way of communicating this news. If the helper cannot recognize that this information belongs to the patient and no one else, it may mean that the professional has been "hooked" by his or her own personal experiences. For example, the family care provider may not have been told that a loved one was dying. Unless the helper has found a way to reach some resolution about this experience, these unfinished personal feelings can damage the present helping process. The helper can load his or her personal agenda and anger onto the patient's situation and become angry at the patient for the lack of open communication and the inability to cope with unfinished business. The question is: *whose* unfinished business?

Sam is an eighty-four year old retired carpenter who now has AIDS due to a blood transfusion he had six years ago. His health is beginning to fail. He doesn't want anyone to know his diagnosis, not even his children. He has demanded that his wife and health care professionals not tell them. He insists on telling his children that he has leukemia.

Certainly the challenge for the helping professional is to recognize how personal experiences can negatively influence the art of the helping process. It is obvious in this example that if the helper were to try to force the patient to disclose the diagnosis to his children, the relationship between the helper and the patient would quickly come to an end. Sometimes the obvious is not always clear to us when we are thrust into the middle of such a complicated situation. The most supportive thing that the helper could do in this situation is to respect the patient's wishes and provide ongoing support, information, and advocacy so that current and future care needs are met.

PARENTS

The largest number of older adults affected by the HIV epidemic are the parents of those who are ill, who have died, and who are yet to be diagnosed (Riley, Ory, & Zablotsky, 1989). Parents of people with HIV illness are a diverse group who live in all regions of the country. They span several generations and have a variety of religions, political affiliations, and cultural heritages. Parents vary greatly in the level of support that they can physically, emotionally, and financially offer their adult children. There may be competition for resources between parents and their children. Retired parents frequently have limited incomes, and the physical health of parents varies greatly.

Many parents experience the double trauma of finding out that their son is gay at the same time they learn of his illness. A parent's first discovery of his or her child's homosexuality often includes a grieving process (Skeen, Walters, & Robinson, 1988). Initially, parents are likely to feel shock and anger. Frequently, they feel sadness and loss at the prospect of not having a son or daughter who will marry and have children. Usually, parents are able to move through this process and reach some acceptance of having a gay or lesbian child. If the parents find out at the same time that their son is gay and also has AIDS, they are likely to experience a double load of grief and loss. If the parents have known that their son is gay and now find out that he has AIDS, the earlier grief is likely to be reignited. Despite going through this often complicated grieving process, many parents provide enormous levels of support to their adult children who may be seriously or terminally ill. Unfortunately, other parents have not been able to come to terms with having a gay son and, therefore, cannot assist the son through this transition. The social context and the level of social supports available to parents in different geographic locales vary significantly. These factors vary and are major influences in the parents' coping abilities.

Helen lived in the southeastern part of the United States. When her son, Michael, developed AIDS and got progressively more ill, she began to get increasingly anxious that he would want to move back from California to be cared for by her. She loved her son deeply and wanted to take care of him, but was very conflicted because she didn't want anyone to know that Michael had AIDS. She was fearful of the social climate in her town because children with AIDS there had been objects of hatred and discrimination. She resolved the conflict by closing up her home and moving to California to care for Michael until he died, four months later. Several months after her return home, Helen sought grief counseling because she was feeling so isolated. It was difficult for her to find a grief counselor who was sensitive and supportive of her needs.

Helper Response: Empathy Versus Anger

There are a variety of responses by care providers toward the parents of a person with HIV illness. Many of these responses are colored by the helping professional's relationship with his or her own parents. For instance, the helper's experience with parental intimacy or conflict may be reenacted in the client helping process. It is human to identify with a family member. It is often a difficult challenge to keep clear of such alliances. Helpers may feel deep compassion for the psychological struggles of the parents. Conversely, helpers may feel anger toward the parents for their rejection of their seriously ill son. The grief counselor Helen consulted after her return home could not provide appropriate counseling because she had intense negative judgments about homosexuality. The mature role for a helper in such a situation is to refer the client to another counselor, or to do some personal exploration about his or her own homophobia.

DEMENTIA

One aspect of HIV illness that is strikingly similar to the diseases common among older people is AIDS dementia complex (ADC). Also known as HIV cognitive impairment (HCI), its symptoms somewhat resemble Alzheimer's disease.

A person with HIV cognitive loss requires much the same type of supervision and protection that a person with Alzheimer's needs. Watching the cognitive deterioration of a loved one is a tormenting process of letting go. Those close to the individual with HIV cognitive impairment or Alzheimer's feel a deep sense of loss long before death actually occurs. An unfortunate combination of circumstances occurs when both the older parent and adult child have lost cognitive abilities.

Helper Response: Unearthed Grief

If the helping professional has ever experienced the cognitive deterioration of a loved one, the encounter with HIV cognitive impairment is sure to awaken an array of feelings from that earlier time. It is doubly difficult if the helper has unresolved feelings about having had to place a parent with Alzheimer's or other dementia in a nursing home. The helper may find him- or herself drifting back emotionally to this earlier time, unable to focus on the situation at hand. Because this type of loss is so painful to witness, care providers sometimes unwittingly collude with the patient in minimizing the actual extent of mental status changes. Or they wait for a person with dementia to make decisions he or she cannot make. Objectivity is lost and patient advocacy cannot follow. Seeking a neuropsychiatric consultation to assess the patient's functioning will help care providers in formulating an appropriate plan of care.

AIDS AND SUICIDE

Clinical experience, as well as documentation in various parts of the country, reflects the fact that gestures and thoughts of suicide, as well as completed suicides, are fairly common among people with HIV illness (Goldblum & Moulton, 1989). Care providers will confront these issues with greater frequency as the HIV epidemic continues. In geographic areas hit hard by the epidemic, reminders of mortality are often difficult to escape. In New York, Los Angeles, and San Francisco, many gay men have lost not only partners, but also many friends. Care providers in these regions have come in contact with surviving partners of people who have died from AIDS. These partners are often ill themselves. Survivors who have sustained multiple losses, or who have witnessed the devastation of HIV illness in a loved one, may think about suicide if they begin to get sick. Thoughts and expressions of suicide often signify an attempt to seek and maintain control over one's destiny. Arguments can be made for what constitutes a cry for help versus a rational suicide (Siegel, 1986), but the professional helper needs first to be very clear about his or her countertransference issues around suicide (see Chapter 3).

Helper Responses: Helplessness Versus Competence

The patient's thoughts, feelings, and discussions about suicide can easily threaten the professional's sense of being able to help. (For more on suicide, see Chapter 3, Effective Intervention and Negative Emotional Reactions to Suicidal Elders.) Helpers often feel anxious, panicked, and powerless in such situations. It is a challenge to remain supportive, attentive, and objective when a client begins to talk about suicide. Because this is such an emotionally charged topic, a professional can be seduced into minimizing these thoughts and feelings in the client as an unconscious means of protecting him- or herself. On the other hand, a care provider may identify with the client to such a degree that he or she is unable to objectively assess the client's risk for suicide or the particular meaning that the thoughts, feelings, or plans for suicide hold for that individual. The helper may feel that he or she would consider the same option should a similar situation arise in his or her life. On the other extreme, an AIDS-phobic or homophobic helper may feel that the client's suicide would be a just outcome. Care providers therefore need to confront their own anxieties about death, as well as their biases about suicide, to avoid either over- or under-reacting. It is usually wise for the helper to seek consultation or supervision in order to be better prepared to assess risk for suicide and to avoid emotional pitfalls in the helping process.

AIDS AND BEREAVEMENT

There are now more survivors of people with HIV illness than there are people who have actually died from the disease. The survivors include gay and bisexual men and women, sexual partners of injection drug users, spouses and partners of blood transfusion recipients, parents, siblings, members of extended families, and friends. The survivors are as unique and diverse as the people who have died. Certain issues are likely to confront survivors of someone who has died from AIDS (O'Neil, 1987; Pheifer & Houseman, 1988). These include: the need for secrecy about the cause of death, the lack of institutional sanctioning for same sex relationships, lack of appropriate grieving rituals for a death due to AIDS, internalized homophobia, multiple losses, poor health of the surviving partner, and the fatigue from care giving and stigmatization. Specialized support services are needed for survivors of an HIV-related death. These services include support groups, individual grief counseling and therapy, community rituals, national expressions of mourning (such as the NAMES Project Quilt), social activism, and education.

Helper Response: Empathy Versus Grief Overload

To be able to provide effective grief counseling and support, the helping professional needs to be in touch with his or her own feelings about death, loss and grief, and AIDS. If the helper has been fortunate enough to have not yet experienced a personal loss, he or she may not be able to identify what loss feels like. He or she is therefore limited in offering empathic support to the bereaved. If the helper is a member of the gay or lesbian community or a recovering substance abuser, he or she is likely to have known many people who are either currently sick or have died. *Grief overload* describes this situation. The helper becomes so saturated by HIV-related deaths that there may be little emotional reserve available to support others through the painful process of grief and mourning.

Implications for Practice

Aging and AIDS challenge the helping professional's emotional resources and abilities to cope with illness, decline, debilitation, and death. What then do we need in order to continue to do the work of helping others through an often extraordinary process of change? Perhaps the biggest need is the opportunity to reflect on what we are doing as helpers and how we are affected by it. Many agencies offer support groups for staff to create an opportunity to talk about the emotional impact of providing help. This can ease the sense of isolation that we may feel in the course of our work. One challenge is to view countertransference issues not as stumbling blocks, but as opportunities to refine our skills. One of the distinctly human qualities of the helping process is the mirror that it often holds up to our souls. We learn much about ourselves in the process of helping others, and AIDS/HIV illness offers an exceptional learning experience for practitioners.

Some specific strategies we can develop to learn and benefit from countertransference, when it arises in caring for older people affected by HIV illness, include the following:

1. Identify countertransference when it happens. This means paying attention to what is happening to us in the process of helping. Spend a few moments at the end of the day reflecting on how the day went. What was difficult about it? What was challenging?
2. Acknowledge that our feelings and reactions are real and require our attention. Sometimes, as we have seen, reactions may have very little to do with our client's experience. Are we responding to what is being said to us, or are we reminded of our own experiences and feelings that are awakened in the present helping process?
3. Anticipate where we are going with the client. What might our next encounter with the client be like? This strategy helps to keep us focused on the client's need. At the same time, it keeps us aware of our own feelings.

Helpers are deeply affected by the art and process of helping another. Sometimes we are more aware of how we are affected than other times. As human beings, we are also deeply affected by our own personal relationships and experiences. Sometimes our personal and professional experiences may flow into one another like the branches of a river. The challenge for us is to recognize where the river begins, from which sources its channels flow, and what it sounds like when it is flowing at full force.

Summary

AIDS and aging confront the helping professional with many similar problems. When working with older adults with HIV illness, the most common blocks to effective helping are ageism; AIDS phobia, homophobia; and the fear of illness, decline, and death. Effective strategies to cope with these blocks include being aware and paying attention to our feelings, utilizing our feelings to learn more about the art and process of helping others, and adapting our professional behaviors as a result of understanding our countertransference reactions.

References

Catania, J., Turner, H., Kegles, S., Stall, R., Pollack, L., & Coates, T. (1989). Older Americans and AIDS: Transmission risks and primary prevention research needs. *The Gerontologist, 29*(3), 373-381.

Goldblum, P., & Moulton, J. (1989). HIV disease and suicide. In J. Dilley, C. Pies, & M. Helquist (Eds.), *Face to face: A guide to AIDS counseling* (pp. 152-164). San Francisco: AIDS Health Project, University of California.

O'Neil, M. (1987). AIDS and bereavement: Partners, families and friends. In P. Franks, A. Hughes, & J. Martin (Eds.), *AIDS home care and hospice manual.* San Francisco, CA: Visiting Nurse Association.

Pheifer, W. C., & Houseman, C. (1988). Bereavement and AIDS: A framework for intervention. *Journal of Psychosocial Nursing, 26*(10), 21-26.

Riley, M. W., Ory, M. G., & Zablotsky, D. (Eds.) (1989). *AIDS in an aging society: What we need to know.* New York: Springer.

Siegel, K. (1986). Psychosocial aspects of rational suicide. *American Journal of Psychotherapy, 15,* 405-418.

Skeen, P., Walters, L., & Robinson, B. (1988). How parents of gays react to their children's homosexuality and to the threat of AIDS. *Journal of Psychosocial Nursing, 26*(12), 7-10.

5

Disability and the Personal-Professional Connection

MARVIN L. ROSENBERG, JR.

We who work with disabled people are guaranteed to have a multitude of personal feelings and reactions as we confront people whose activity, relationships, and abilities have been altered by disability. We are challenged to look into ourselves and wonder if we could, or would want to, continue living if we suddenly found ourselves in our clients' situations. Our personal feelings toward our clients and our clients' disabilities can influence our ability to provide them help and have a great influence on our personal satisfaction.

Disability is the chronic or permanent loss of psychological and/or physiological function due to either organic or external forces. The degree of disability or the rate of its progression may exceed the normal aging process, or it may represent a lower level of functioning than is socially expected. In this way, disabled people are often "instantly old."

Self-Awareness Test

To better understand the personal-professional connection as it relates to disability, we must be willing to explore our own feelings. Our feelings surrounding a particular type of disability and disabled client will influence the help we can provide. Feelings that elude us, or that we experience in an exaggerated or diminished way, may compromise our helping relationships. *The Self-Awareness Test* (see Table 5.1) provides a way to get in touch with the kinds and intensity of feelings you have toward various disabilities. If you have unacknowledged or unmanaged feelings toward a particular type of disability, it is very possible they will be transferred to your clients. For example, my stepmother and mother both died of cancer that wasted away their bodies. When I think about this and see someone in a similar situation, it brings up my feelings of hopelessness, helplessness, and fear. If I were unaware of these feelings, or did not keep them in mind when working with other cancer patients, I could end up behaving toward my patients as I did toward my mother and stepmother. I could begin to re-enact my own helplessness and hopelessness in a way that would not be useful to my clients.

Please consider how you would feel if you, a close friend, or a family member had each type of disability described in Table 5.1 below. The five-point scale is provided to allow you to experience the intensity of your feelings about each type of disability.

Helpers whose feelings in a given situation fall to either end of the scale (1 or 5) are more vulnerable to countertransferential difficulty. If a particular client's situation causes us to feel very anxious, sad, or helpless, we may avoid the situation and the client. Conversely, if we feel little or no anxiety, helplessness, or sadness about a particular client's situation, we may also avoid or ignore the client's needs. Another possibility arises when, for some reason, we feel particularly sorry or solicitous of particular clients and their situations. In this case, we may either be drawn to the clients or attempt to avoid them. Our personal feelings influence how we define and carry out our helping role.

Table 5.1 The Self-Awareness Test

Type of Disability	Least				Most
	(anxious, sad, helpless, solicitous)				
1. Watching your body waste away inch by inch.	1	2	3	4	5
2. Losing bladder or bowel control.	1	2	3	4	5
3. Having no feeling or muscle use in your body from your neck down.	1	2	3	4	5
4. Being unable to recall who you were or answer simple questions about your past.	1	2	3	4	5
5. Being dependent for bathing, toileting, and being moved from place to place.	1	2	3	4	5
6. Having your face badly scarred or deformed.	1	2	3	4	5
7. Losing your sight and hearing at age 25.	1	2	3	4	5
8. Never being able to do your favorite activity again.	1	2	3	4	5
9. Having an illness where your physical strength fluctuated from hour to hour, to such a degree that you could not rely on yourself to get in and out of bed.	1	2	3	4	5

NOTE: It is natural and normal for all of us to have a wide range of feelings surrounding the situations described above. It is only when those feelings go unnoticed or unmanaged that our ability to get help may be compromised.

Expectational Barriers

As helpers, we place value on providing services that will allow others to live life with greater quality and ease. In theory our professional training taught us to attempt to maintain client objectivity. In practice, however, it is not always clear if our feelings for a disabled client's well-being are based on our personal life experiences and needs or our professional judgment.

Our feelings and beliefs about a disabled client can take the form of expectations both of ourselves as care providers and of the client. These expectational barriers may hinder or compromise care. An *expectational barrier* can be defined as a conscious or unconscious conflict evolving from our personal and professional connection with a client. It causes us to behave, or feel like we want to behave, toward a disabled client in a manner that would be counterproductive. Many kinds of expectational barriers can block the helping process. Two which occur most frequently are practitioners' personal perceptions surrounding disability, and practitioners' expectations surrounding rehabilitation.

PRACTITIONERS' PERCEPTIONS OF DISABILITY

As helpers, our personal expectations surrounding disability come from a combination of messages received from our families, society, and life experiences. Although many of these messages have their foundations in childhood, they are tested, refined, and become a part of our adult life view. These beliefs, or biases, may influence the caregiving relationship in many ways.

For example, when I was a boy my mother was involved in many charitable organizations. As a result a constant stream of older persons, of varying degrees of health, came through our home. I learned very early that aging was not something to fear. There were certain freedoms associated with being old. Physical disability and psychological functioning were not necessarily interrelated. Appliances—such as hearing aids, glasses, canes, leg braces, artificial limbs, and wheelchairs—were a normal part of life. I saw that human beings, regardless of age or psychological or physiological deficits, could be quite ingenious in adapting life to meet their needs successfully.

I evolved a very optimistic view of aging and disability that I once thought would be a great asset to me as a helping professional. What I learned, however, was that my optimism was also a liability; I had a tendency to minimize the emotional impact disability might have on a client. I also had a tendency to see a client's potential for recovery as greater than it might actually have been.

I worked with Tom, a middle-aged divorced man, who, as a result of a job-related injury, had his right leg amputated. Prior to his amputation, he had been healthy and vital. His only exposure to the medical system was an occasional checkup. He had never experienced serious illness or disability in his own family or circle of friends. As we began our counseling relationship, I thought to myself, "He's lucky. With an artificial leg, Tom will be able to return to his job and most of the activities he was accustomed to." Although I was not so bold as to verbally communicate my optimism for his prognosis and rehabilitation, unintentionally and without any awareness, it seeped into our relationship. After several visits, I noticed Tom becoming increasingly more irritable. I thought he was having a hard time managing his grief and the normal fears, inconveniences, and discomfort associated with his hospitalization and rehabilitation. One day toward the end of our session, Tom burst out in anger, "You just don't get it, do you? You come here, do your thing with patients and then go back to the real world of pretty, whole people. You and everyone else around here think this amputation is no big deal. Someone yesterday even told me I was lucky. Damn them! There is nothing lucky about this. No woman is going to want a man like me."

As I continued to listen to Tom, I was struck by how my beliefs about managing life successfully with disability had kept me from really hearing Tom's opposite perspective. I had not only failed to see things from Tom's viewpoint, but I had also never considered that his irritability might have something to do with me.

PRACTITIONERS' EXPECTATIONS OF REHABILITATION

Practitioners' expectations surrounding rehabilitation may also interfere with or complicate the treatment process. Our hopes, wishes, and desires for a disabled person's psychological and physiological wellness may prevent us from seeing his or her true rehabilitation potential.

One morning I overheard Sue, an experienced and normally soft-spoken physical therapist, shouting at Florence, a frail-looking, 85-year-old woman recovering from a broken hip. Florence had fallen at home, where she had been living independently. She was making very slow progress and it was likely that she would be placed in a nursing home. I was disturbed by the harsh way Sue had spoken to Florence. I asked Sue if she would have lunch with me, hoping we could talk about the incident. At lunch, Sue told me she had grown quite attached to Florence, who reminded her of her grandmother. Sue told me her grandmother had died in a nursing home after being unable to recover her independence following a fall at home. She feared Florence would suffer the same fate if she didn't try harder. Sue went on to say it would be very difficult for her to see Florence go to a nursing home.

As I listened, it was obvious Sue had not consciously made the connection between her grandmother and Florence. Sue's growing feelings regarding what had happened to her grandmother were interfering with her relationship with Florence. Sue's personal expectations had caused her to behave in an uncharacteristic fashion and, as it turned out, to overestimate Florence's potential for recovery.

Co-Conspiracy for Denial

Denial is a normal and healthy psychological defense mechanism. It protects us from an intensity of emotional pain which, if experienced all at once, would compromise our ability to cope with and manage life. When a disabled person faces sweeping adjustments, there is a normal tendency to avoid confronting issues that generate emotional pain. Helpers, like disabled people, also avoid emotionally painful issues. Some of these issues relate to the helpers' own feelings as they fantasize to themselves what it might be like to be disabled, like their client. Other issues stem from the helper's need to protect or shield the disabled person from emotional pain. Still others may relate to recollections of something or someone in the helper's personal life that are triggered by the disabled person. Often, the result is that both the helper and the disabled person avoid certain tasks or topics of discussion necessary for successful rehabilitation and adjustment.

Marge, a 64-year-old woman, was brought to our hospital after suffering a stroke. The stroke left her with a mild speech impediment and some paralysis of her right leg and arm. Bill, Marge's husband of 30 years, attended all her therapy sessions. Bill and I had several private conversations, as did

Marge and I, about the many aspects of rehabilitation. We also had two joint sessions to attempt to address concerns they both had. I thought we had covered everything. Marge called me to her room the last day she was in the hospital. After a brief exchange she said, "What about sex? Is it safe? Do you have any suggestions of how I might talk to Bill, for we are going to have to make some adjustments?" I was taken off guard by her questions. It wasn't because I was uncomfortable talking about sex. I had routinely raised the subject during the rehabilitation of younger stroke victims. I was, however, not accustomed to discussing anything sexual with people my parents' age or older. I suddenly felt embarrassed and began to blush. Marge looked at me and said, "I didn't mean to embarrass you. You're the person I feel the most comfortable talking with. I just haven't been ready to discuss this until now!"

I went on to address her questions and concerns. After our session, I asked myself why I hadn't addressed the topic of sexuality and intimacy with Marge or Bill. I realized that my personal discomfort had gotten in the way. Marge and Bill had also not felt comfortable. All three of us had conspired to successfully avoid the topic.

Practitioner Fears

Being helpers for disabled persons means continually placing ourselves in situations that challenge and confront our personal sense of security and well-being. Our clients are a constant reminder that bad things, which suddenly and drastically change people's lives and their relationships, can happen. As helpers, it is not possible to avoid our fear that we could be in our client's situation. Each of us has developed characteristic ways of managing fear. Some of us become irritable, angry, and combative. Others retreat and become sad or depressed.

Have you or one of your colleagues ever left a client feeling enraged and been unable to figure out why? Possibly you have found yourself arguing with a client for no good reason. Conversely, you may have felt devastated, sad, or depressed after working with a client. These feelings can have their foundation in many areas of the personal-professional connection. They may be normal and appropriate responses to a client's situation. However when our personal fears, triggered by our professional connections, go unacknowledged or unmanaged, we risk compromising our helping.

The Self-Awareness Test at the beginning of this chapter can provide each of us a clearer idea of the basis of our personal fears related to disability. The four losses most commonly feared by helpers working with disabled persons are (1) loss of physical independence, (2) loss of emotional support, (3) loss of control over one's self and life, and (4) loss of our ability to attain and maintain physical and emotional intimacy.

It can be helpful to examine each of these four areas of fear. Think of clients you have been involved with. Did these fears surface for you? How did you handle them? Did you discuss them with your clients? Did you discuss them with your supervisor, colleagues, close friends, or family? One of the ways we can best help our clients is to acknowledge our personal fears of disability. One of the best ways to handle our personal fears is to keep them in mind and to talk them through with someone.

Unresolved Grief Work

Throughout life we are continuously trying and experiencing new things and giving up old ones. When we work with disabled clients, we naturally become attached. We care not only for them but about them. Our work requires that we form attachments for brief periods of time and then let them go. Often disabled clients get better, and no longer require our services; or they get worse and require intensified efforts to help. Some clients transfer to nursing homes; others die. In all of these cases, we find ourselves suddenly separated from people we have grown to care about. Western society does not support helpers taking the time or energy often required to grieve over these relationships. It simply says: "You've done your job, now let go and attach yourself to the next client and begin the helping process again." Each of us must grieve for these lost relationships, or eventually we will lose our capacity to start and maintain new ones. We may have a very difficult time letting go of present clients if we have not adequately grieved over losing the preceding ones. (See also Chapter 2.)

Inappropriate Termination

When we begin a helping relationship with a disabled person, we are given many responsibilities. We must use our intuition, life experience, education, and skill to build a relationship that fosters trust, confidence, independence, and permission for our clients to accept our help. We often must take the lead in establishing the structure of the relationship, deciding what will be done, when it will be done, and how it will be done. Further, we must decide how much we will allow the client to become physically and emotionally dependent on us and our relationship with them and when and how to re-establish the client's independence. For these reasons, helping relationships have the unique quality of beginning unequally. The helper has something the disabled person needs or requires, and the disabled person may have only a limited ability to reciprocate. This imbalance is often at the crux of a range of feelings that surface in the helper and the disabled person. It is not uncommon for the disabled person to experience feeling like a burden, emotionally indebted to the helper, hopeless, or like a failure. On the other hand, as helpers, we may experience feeling drained, imposed upon, used, and manipulated. Both the helper and the disabled person may feel that neither could function without the other. When these feelings develop, persist, and are ignored, the helping relationship becomes dysfunctional. Often the result is that the helper and the disabled person sever the relationship in an inappropriate or premature fashion.

Jerry, a 24-year-old man paralyzed from the neck down after a hang gliding accident, was undergoing rehabilitation in the hospital. Jerry had been doing well during his first month of rehabilitation. One afternoon I received a message that Jerry urgently needed to talk to me. I went to his room to find him very upset, saying; "I have had it with that _____ nurse; Sandy promised three days ago to bring me some recording tape and still hasn't done it. She's not been answering my calls

for help and yesterday didn't come to put me on the commode, even though I had reminded her, and I messed the bed.
I think she is avoiding me. We had been getting along so well.
Maybe we were getting along too well! I was beginning to feel
strongly for her. After all, I guess it's true, nobody wants to
be around a helpless cripple." I asked Jerry what, if anything,
he wanted me to do about the situation. Jerry told me he
wanted me to keep Sandy from providing any more of his
care.

I left him and found Sandy, who was also angry and exas-
perated. She stated, "I've given Jerry my best shot. A couple
of days ago he began to make inappropriate sexual comments
to me in front of his roommate and his roommate's family. I
felt humiliated, and at a loss to discuss this with him. I keep
forgetting to bring in some recording tape I promised him,
and the way I feel now I wish I hadn't volunteered to do it in
the first place. I'm trying to spend as little time as I can with
him, and when I do, I just tend to business. That hasn't seemed
to help much; he seems to have just gotten more demanding.
Yesterday I'd had it up to here with him (putting her hand
above her head), and missed getting him up on the commode.
He had a B.M. in the bed. I felt so bad because I know how
shy and easily embarrassed he is. It was my fault, but I have
my limits, too.

Let us look more closely at Sandy's personal-professional connections with Jerry. Sandy had been nursing approximately three
years and was 26 years old. She told me she had been attracted to
Jerry almost from the beginning because of his wit and gentleness.
She stated that her feelings were platonic, like those she felt
toward her brothers, whom she missed since moving across the
country to take this job. Gradually, over the month, Sandy's sis-
terly feelings for Jerry had caused her to expand the helping
relationship to include more than basic caregiving. Jerry was
becoming increasingly dependent on her for special favors and
emotional support. Although Sandy said she sensed Jerry might
be developing romantic feelings toward her, she wasn't certain.
She was reluctant to talk with him about this. She felt it might
result in another blow to his self-esteem, and she felt uncomfortable discussing attraction with her patients. Sandy began to see

that Jerry was becoming quite dependent on her. She knew in the long run this would not help him but she didn't know what to do, except pull back. Her pulling back just happened to coincide with Jerry's growing feelings for her, resulting in the collapse of this caregiving relationship. Sandy's warm personal feelings for Jerry had caused her to step outside of her professional role, creating an interaction that resulted in both Sandy and Jerry wanting to terminate their relationship.

Personal attraction may arise between helpers and disabled clients of any age (see Chapter 11). Nurturing can slide easily into affectional and sexual feelings. However, it is seldom appropriate for professionals to act on their own sexual feelings or to encourage disabled clients to act on theirs. Sometimes, as in the case of Sandy and Jerry, a third party can be helpful. Jerry admitted his attraction to Sandy. I explained to him that the kind of remarks he was making were not appropriate in a hospital setting. Sandy stopped doing extra things for Jerry, and concentrated on providing nursing care. They both agreed to continue to talk about their personal-professional relationship.

Summary

Helpers' personal feelings toward disability and disabled clients can not only interfere with the helping relationship, but derail it altogether. The Self-Awareness Test provides a tool to discover your personal feelings toward many disabling situations. Some of the more common problems that arise result from our own expectational barriers, co-conspiracy for denial, fears around disability, unresolved grief, and inappropriate termination.

It is perfectly normal for helpers to have a wide range of personal feelings for clients. It is only when we ignore or deny them that they have the possibility to escape our managing them in an appropriate fashion. One of the significant challenges in our role as helpers, regardless of how many years of experience we may have, is discovering and understanding our feelings surrounding the personal-professional connection—countertransference. When we do this successfully, our reward is ongoing personal and professional growth and satisfaction.

References

Brenman Pick, I. (1985). Working through the countertransference. *International Journal Psycho-Analysis, 66,* 157-166.

Evans, R. L., Halar, E., DeFreece, A. B., & Larson, G. L. (1976, May). Multidisciplinary approach to sex education of spinal cord injured patients. *Physical Therapy, 56*(5), 541-545.

Katz, V., Gordon, R., Iverson, D., & Meyers, S. J. (1978-1979). Past histories of depression in parapalegic individuals. *Parapalegia, 15,* 8-14.

Kowalsky, E. L. (1978, March). Grief: A lost life style. *American Journal of Nursing,* 418-420.

Weller, D. V., & Miller, P. M. (1977, Summer). Emotional reactions of patient, family, and staff in acute-care period of spinal cord injury: Part I. *Social Work in Health Care, 2*(4), 369-377.

6

Facing the Loss of What Makes Us Uniquely Human: Working with Dementia Patients

EDITH S. KAPLAN

A woman comes to a psychologist with a complicated presentation of memory loss, depression and anxiety. The psychologist treats the depression and anxiety without acknowledging his patient's cognitive decline because it is too painful for him to accept her deterioration. This denial affects his goals and interventions with this patient. Through supervision, he realizes that the patient reminds him of what his mother would

AUTHOR'S NOTE: I would like to gratefully acknowledge all the people who generously shared their thoughts and feelings with me. Their openness and honesty provided a rich and valuable contribution to this chapter.

be like if she were still alive. "Saving" the patient is, in essence, like saving his own mother from death and saving himself from having to lose her.

An occupational therapist at an adult day health center admits feeling angry at a disruptive patient and wonders if the program can continue to manage him. She recalls that she felt angry at a similar program years ago when her father, a victim of stroke, was turned away as "too difficult." She now feels the same frustration those other workers had most likely experienced with her father. She also understands firsthand the problems disruptive patients present in this setting.

A nurse's aide, who visits Alzheimer's patients in their homes, feels frustrated when she tries to talk with them. This is mild compared to her difficulty in discussing patients' diagnoses with them. She fears an angry, negative response and relates this to trying to cope with an unpredictable alcoholic parent in her own growing up years. At that time, she developed a deep fear of anger and a survival mechanism of avoidance. Yet, ethically, she believes in patients' rights to know their diagnoses.

All staff at an assessment center respond with fear and sadness to an especially poignant case of a 55-year-old man, with a new wife and small child, whom they diagnose with early Alzheimer's. They work hard to find some treatable cause for the memory decline in this man in the prime of life. It is too painful to contemplate his deterioration and its effect on his young family; and it is too close for comfort for staff themselves, many of whom are either in, or entering, their own middle years. Overidentification with the patient's misfortune (Hiatt, cited in Nemiroff & Colarusso, 1985), however, interferes with staff's ability to realistically assess the possibilities and communicate effectively to his family.

Working with clients who have dementia can raise deep emotions, because dementia compromises much of what makes us unique as human beings. While all species in the animal kingdom have brains, only humans have a mind, a process that gives us the ability to be conscious of self, to be aware of time and place in the world, and to develop a spoken language. These abilities, along with memory, allow us to go beyond the present, to relate ourselves to the past and project ourselves into the future (Public Broadcasting System, 1988). With dementia, however, all our most human capabilities can be lost: cognition, memory, judgment, perception, and speech. People lose, in varying degrees, the ability to perform their normal daily activities, to care for themselves and others, and to communicate and interact effectively. While numerous conditions cause dementia, the term used in this chapter refers to Alzheimer's disease and Multi-Infarct Dementia, the two major causes of dementia in the elderly today. The characteristics and courses of these diseases differ somewhat, but both are severely disabling.

A wide range of practitioners—doctors, nurses, psychologists, social workers, occupational therapists—work with dementia patients in a variety of settings: physician offices, hospitals, outpatient clinics, home care agencies, adult day health centers, nursing homes, and others. They come face to face with people who are old, cognitively and mentally impaired, physically and functionally disabled, and dying. Any one of these conditions is enough to stir up feelings in professionals. Confronting all of these conditions (often all present in one person) can create even more intense reactions. As practitioners, we are forced to confront the tragic loss of abilities earlier in our lives than we normally would have; at the same time, our anxiety is raised by our clients being nearer to death (Knight, 1986).

Work with dementia patients most often involves dealing with family members as well, adding another dimension. As practitioners and as human beings we bring with us feelings about ourselves and our parents, grandparents, and significant others. Whether or not we are aware of these feelings—or experience them directly—they influence our work. Getting acquainted with these feelings in both their positive and negative aspects, and learning to use them constructively, can significantly affect our work and also be of great personal value.

Common Reactions and Behaviors

Practitioners working with dementia patients often experience feelings of sadness, frustration, helplessness, and fear that it will happen to us. In some settings, we must cope with difficult behaviors such as wandering, combativeness, and inappropriate sexuality. Our patients may have regressed to an infantile level, requiring staff to feed, dress, and toilet them. These behaviors and demands can try our patience, raise doubts about the value of our efforts, and call our competence into question.

In addition to reactions to patients, we must also keep in mind the two other points in the aging triangle (see Chapter 1). First, we have our own reactions to our own aging processes (vis-à-vis bodily changes, significant losses, appreciation of life's limitations, and death anxiety). Second, we have our reactions to our own parents and significant others, who may be the age of our patients and dealing with similar life tasks (Nemiroff & Colarusso, 1985).

Bringing into awareness the particular feelings that influence each of us is necessary to good practice. Otherwise, we risk behaving in ways that are not in the patient's best interest. For example, fearing our own helplessness, we may deny patients' real conditions and either expect too much from them or do too much for them. I sometimes catch myself being maternal or overly solicitous with patients who seem particularly emotionally or physically vulnerable, tapping into the overprotective role I learned early in my own family. Because this behavior can be almost automatic for me, I need to remind myself that each patient must be viewed objectively and "taking care of them" is not always the most appropriate response.

We also need to look at how our feelings and biases affect our views of family members of dementia patients. These feelings can distort how we relate to them and influence our recommendations regarding care of the older person, placement decisions, legal and financial arrangements, counseling, and other services. For example, a number of practitioners report feeling like an ideal child (Hiatt, cited in Nemiroff & Colarusso, 1985). They compete with the patient's own adult children, seeing the patient in a very positive light, while the real children have more realistic mixed feelings. The professional then takes the side of the patient and feels superior to the children, behaving like the perfect child to a perfect parent and leaving the real children in the role of bad or neglectful kids. The danger here is that these feelings may prevent a realistic appraisal of and empathy for the family members' situation and may be inappropriately communicated to them in the work.

When nursing home placement is an issue, the stakes rise. In discussing countertransference regarding placement in a nursing home, Knight (1986) states:

> Clinicians who have strong personal needs to see their own decisions backed up by the decisions of others may influence . . . families overtly by recommending one or another course of action or may influence the decision more covertly by giving or withholding verbal or nonverbal cues of approval as the client discusses the various options. (p. 148)

Regarding decision making, Knight (1986) goes on to say: "Within the familial context, it is seldom true that only objective factors will be considered. The decisions that are made are often the expression of deeply felt and not well-recognized emotions" (p. 154). This is true for families and practitioners alike. In fact, many countertransference reactions experienced by practitioners are mirrored in families, and vice versa, although not always simultaneously. Consider the following example:

> A primary care physician realizes that she generally takes the position of giving families permission to place their relatives in nursing homes. This relates to her own past family situation, where there was conflict around placing her demented grandmother, who lived in their home. Her father and uncle were against placement, and she, her mother, and her aunt were in favor of it. Thus, she now sees herself as taking this same role with patients' families.

Knight (1986) advises that the practitioner,

> who is aware of strong feelings that one decision or another is the correct one in all cases should seek consultation or supervision in order to work through this blind spot and be able to deal with families as individualized systems. (p. 148)

Recognizing Countertransference

Interviewing other practitioners for this chapter has borne out my own experience that many helpers are unaware of countertransference feelings. Professional training in many disciplines encourages this lack of awareness by emphasizing objectivity, professional distance, and intellectual understanding at the expense of emotional understanding. Freud himself originally recommended "emotional aloofness and coldness" and putting aside all one's own feelings (Menninger & Holzman, 1973). Applying the concept of countertransference to work with the elderly is relatively new but as Hassler (1985) points out, for both the middle-aged and older practitioner and his or her patient, "thoughts and feelings about the finiteness of time and personal death, although disguised, are rarely absent" (p. 115).

How then do we as practitioners become aware of these feelings that can so influence our work? We can begin with self-observation. "The key clues are intense emotional reactions to clients or particular actions of clients or reactions that are atypical" (Knight, 1986, p. 143) for the practitioner. For example, a clinical nurse had an immediate negative reaction to a very demented patient who couldn't talk. When she met the patient's daughter, who expressed anger at her mother's situation, the nurse immediately disliked her, and transferred this dislike back to the patient. She promptly wanted to avoid this case and do as little as possible. The nurse found this perplexing, as this patient seemed no more difficult than some others she'd seen and her usual reaction was a much more positive one of wanting to nurture. In talking about her unusual reaction, she stated that she felt it might have something to do with her family. Exploring it further, she realized, with some surprise, that the patient looked a little like her mother. The idea that her mother could be in such a condition made her angry. From this awareness, she began to understand the daughter's anger, to which she had immediately reacted. She then was able to see a parallel between her own anger and this adult child's anger.

Menninger and Holzman (1973) describe some of the common ways that countertransference makes its appearance in psychoanalytic treatment. I have adapted several of them, which apply to any therapeutic relationship with older people and their families. These include:

- Depressed or uneasy feelings during or after contact with certain patients or family members
- Carelessness in regard to arrangements, for example, forgetting or being late for appointments
- Getting tired during contact
- Unnecessary sharpness in formulation of comments
- Repeatedly experiencing affectionate feelings towards a patient, or going out of your way to do things you wouldn't do for other patients or families
- A compulsive tendency to "hammer away" at certain points, arguing with the patient or family
- An urge to engage in professional gossip concerning a patient or family member
- A sudden increase or decrease of interest in a certain case

Menninger and Holzman (1973) also make some valuable practical suggestions for using countertransference feelings in psychoanalytic treatment. These, too, I have adapted to apply to the range of helping professionals who work with dementia patients:

1. Be alert to countertransference, but don't be intimidated by it. Think about it from time to time, reflecting on its uses as well as its pitfalls. For example, after a particularly frustrating or rewarding interaction with a patient or family, give some thought to what feelings you experienced and how they hindered or helped your work.
2. Try to recognize feelings that enter into your work generally and try to figure out their meaning in light of what you know about yourself personally. For example, suppose that you consistently avoid, or want to avoid, certain patients or family members. Think about or discuss with a trusted colleague what connection this avoidance may have to your own life.
3. When you become aware of countertransference feelings, especially if they are persistent, try to think through the situation and identify what triggers the reaction in you. Is it some specific feature, or act, or words of the patient or family member? Ask yourself, why am I irritated? Why did this come up now? What is happening in my life that could be affecting me now?

In light of these suggestions I would like to emphasize that countertransference reactions are not always solely related to the practitioner's personal and interpersonal issues and experiences. At times the client may evoke a response that is more directly related to the client's state of being. If you must tell a 55-year-old man that he has early Alzheimer's, for example, and the man starts to cry, your feelings of sadness may spring entirely from his situation. It may have nothing to do with your own life or your feelings about your own parents. It can be difficult to pinpoint the origin of your feelings, but we need to keep in mind that we all do "pick up" feeling states from our clients. This is what empathy is all about.

The Need for a Forum

In addition to self-observation, it is necessary to have a forum for talking about and working through these feelings once they do arise. I interviewed practitioners from various disciplines for this chapter. All said they wanted the opportunity to explore the impact of countertransference on their work. Those who had the benefit of supervision or consultation found it a valuable forum for dealing with countertransference; but the majority of those I spoke with reported having no opportunity available to discuss these feelings. They found our interview very useful in itself and appreciated having this chance to explore their reactions, gain insight about clients and themselves, and take this knowledge back to their work. As one worker put it, "I need to know that these feelings are normal and that other people experience them too."

It is up to each practitioner in the field of gerontology to see to it that opportunities for talking about countertransference feelings are created. This may occur through individual supervision, small group consultation, professional support groups, larger consultation and training sessions, or some combination of these. Whatever the medium, one thing is clear: In order to be competent helpers we need to explore the relationship between countertransference and dementia. As Waelder put it, "Since we are all partially blind, the best we can do is to support each other so that the vision of one may make up for the myopia of the other, and vice versa" (Waelder, cited in Menninger & Holzman, 1973, p. 94).

A Personal Example

Working with dementia patients and families at an Alzheimer's Disease Diagnostic & Treatment Center, I have become increasingly aware of my own countertransference issues and my "aging triangle" (see Chapter 1). Being in early mid-life, I have been acutely aware of the finiteness of time, have experienced some significant losses, and have experienced my own anxiety about death. My family of origin lives in another part of the country. My mother, who suffers from dementia, is cared for primarily by my father—a significant role reversal for them. My older sister, who lives in the same community, provides secondary support. She exemplifies the struggles of the "sandwich generation," helping out with aging parents while carrying out responsibilities to her own college-age children. Working with dementia patients not only reinforces my fear that I could become demented, but raises my anxiety about how I will eventually be cared for and by whom. Will I someday be placed in one of the very care facilities I am obliged to recommend for patients yet intuitively reject for myself?

In my work with dementia patients, I often have a general sense of sadness. I feel helpless to do anything but relate to them as best I can in the moment. Working primarily with families raises even more complex emotions in me. On any given day, I can experience anger, frustration, impatience, irritation, sadness, and helplessness. I can also feel empathy, concern, admiration, satisfaction, and other positive feelings.

Not surprisingly, I have the most difficulty when the family resembles my own. For example, I worked with a family where the mother was demented, the father was primary caregiver, and there were two adult daughters, one of whom lived in another country. The daughter who lived near the couple was most like myself. She had worked in the health services field, was very aware of available resources, and was trying to get her father to accept outside assistance. During the interview, my heartbeat quickened and I became aware of my frustration with the father. The tone of my voice became tinged with impatience, and I began to hammer away at him to convince him he needed in-home help. I noticed I was overidentified with this daughter, and just as frustrated with her father as I was with my own. I was highly interested in having this family follow the daughter's suggestions, but even more so, my own.

After the interview, I thought about the intensity of my reaction to this family. The parallels to my own family were glaring. The daughter was concerned about her father's overburden, just as I was with my own father. She felt strongly about what was needed, as did I (both in this family's situation and my own), and she hammered away at her points. It struck me that she and I were *competing* to see who could get "Dad" to listen. Maybe my struggle with the daughter illustrated my need to feel more powerful as a professional as well as re-playing some of the competition that went on with my own sister. Then, too, perhaps this daughter and I felt so strongly about in-home help due to our guilt about not providing enough direct help ourselves.

As I reviewed all of this, I reminded myself that there are real reasons why caregivers resist outside help: denial, an independent spirit, reluctance to have strangers in the house, and personal needs to maintain caregiver roles. Then I challenged myself to remember that people do not make changes until *they* are ready to do so. By keeping this in mind when the warning signs appear, I am often able to talk to myself, slow things down, and approach situations more objectively. I can then better empathize with families, present available alternatives, and let go of the need to have people do what I think is most sensible. Facing these issues has improved my work with older people and families and eased my relationship with my own family as well.

Positive Countertransference Reactions

The literature on countertransference and this chapter, thus far, have focused on the negative aspects of countertransference. However, practitioners also report very positive feelings about their work. Decisions to work in the field of gerontology seem for some to have grown out of positive feelings toward, and relationships with, elderly people in their own families; for others it has been a desire to work with grandparents they never had; still others speak of the idea that there is much to be learned from this population. Additionally, practitioners report feeling fondly toward dementia patients; feeling satisfied in being able to improve the quality of their lives, if only for a short period of time; and feeling that something valuable is being transmitted between them. As one family practice doctor put it: "Older people have things to teach me, whether or not they're demented. It's hard to put into words, but I get some wisdom from them, some observation about living that will be beneficial to me." A nurse, reflecting on a home visit with a stroke patient, said that although it is hard to see concrete results, she feels that her work is somehow valuable at the time and she experiences an intangible sense of giving and receiving. Our work with this population then is not only a service to them, but can benefit us personally as well.

Some helpers report the ability to recall and respect who the person with dementia once was, either by virtue of their own family experience or from having worked with patients over time. This awareness can be extremely helpful when patients can no longer tell their own stories.

> In this regard, we all have a compound history, a two-faceted history—a history of ourselves as we know it and a history of ourselves as others know it. Not to be known by others, to be in effect without a history by being unable to convey one's past, puts a person at a severe disadvantage in eliciting the understanding and empathy of others; a competitive edge has been lost. (Cohen, 1985, p. 202)

To regain some of this edge, Cohen (1985), who had first seen an 80-year-old woman in psychotherapy and successfully treated her for depression, conveyed a sense of her history to the staff of the nursing home where she resided following a major stroke. This "biography" of his former patient helped the staff to feel more in touch with the patient and to better understand some of the fragmented thoughts she expressed. Cohen went on to develop the idea of putting patients' histories on audio or video cassette, utilizing family members, as a way of presenting changing shifts in the nursing homes with easy access to this information. Cohen's involvement with staff on behalf of the residents with dementia illustrates how he translated his positive countertransference feelings into real quality of care. This kind of creativity can serve as a model to us all.

An adult daughter felt angry that no one in her mother's nursing home knew the woman her mother had been prior to her diagnosis of Alzheimer's. So the daughter posted a huge sheet of paper entitled "This is your life, Mary" on the wall of her mother's room. It listed all of the remarkable things Mary had done between 1892 and 1985: florist, first woman to buy a car in 1913, lead role in a stage play, business woman who opened her own store before World War I, charmer and friend of animals and children. This list helped pin an identity to the frail, confused little woman whom the staff did not know at all. Mary was delighted even though she could not always respond. Some staff members now asked her about being an actress or a florist, instead of why she had rung her bell again, or why she hadn't finished her pudding.

Family members are not the only ones who can create a past history for patients with dementia. Professionals like Cohen model for us how our positive countertransference can reinforce human identity in those patients who have no family and cannot express who they are without help.

Summary

Exploring our countertransference reactions can improve our work with dementia patients and their families. It can also contribute to our own personal growth. Dementia confronts us with the loss of what is most uniquely human, and it therefore provokes strong and complex emotional reactions. Techniques used by psychoanalysts to recognize and deal with countertransference can be adapted to our work with dementia patients and their families.

Self-observation is useful to heighten our self-awareness, but it is not enough. Professionals who work with dementia patients want and need supervision, consultation, and training to explore countertransference feelings. Not all of our countertransference feelings are negative; finding ways to explore the positive feelings as well as the negative ones can only lead to higher quality of care for dementia patients and provide invaluable information for the practitioner.

References

Cohen, G. (1985). Psychotherapy with an eighty-year-old patient. In R. Nemiroff &
C. Colarusso (Eds.), *The race against time* (pp. 195-204). New York: Plenum.
Hassler, J. (1985). Turning forty in analysis. In R. Nemiroff & C. Colarusso (Eds.),
The race against time (pp. 97-115). New York: Plenum.
Hiatt, H. (1971). Dynamic psychotherapy with the aging patient. *American Journal
of Psychotherapy, 25,* 591-600. Quoted in R. Nemiroff and C. Colarusso, (Eds.) *The
race against time.* New York: Plenum.
Knight, B. (1986). *Psychotherapy with older adults.* Beverly Hills, CA: Sage.
Menninger, K., & Holzman, P. (1973) *Theory of psychoanalytic technique.* New York:
Basic Books.
Nemiroff, R., & Colarusso, C. (Eds.) (1985). *The race against time.* New York: Plenum.
Public Broadcasting System. (1988). *The mind, Part 1.* San Francisco, CA: Author.

7

Unhooking:
Co-Dependence, Substance Abuse,
and Countertransference

JEANNE ROBINSON

The Co-Dependent Professional

Professionals who are unaware of their own co-dependency may face problems with countertransference when they work with clients who abuse alcohol or other substances. Originally, *co-dependence* was defined as the behavior pattern of the alcoholic's spouse or significant other. Similar behavior patterns, which are found among people who grew up in alcoholic families, or in families with other types of dysfunction such as mental illness, are also described as co-dependence. These behavior patterns are also found among people whose lives touch those of alcoholics in other ways.

In *Co-Dependence, Misunderstood-Mistreated*, Schaef (1986) stated that

> everyone who works with, lives with, or is around an alcoholic (or a person actively in an addictive process) is by definition a co-dependent and a practicing co-dependent. This includes therapists, counselors, ministers, colleagues, and the family. (p. 29)

Beattie (1987) defined a co-dependent person as: ". . . one who has let another person's behavior affect him or her, and who is obsessed with controlling that person's behavior" (p. 31).

Beattie listed behaviors identified with co-dependency in her book, *Co-Dependent No More* (1987). Her list includes both intrapersonal behaviors, such as feelings of low self-worth, repression, obsession, and denial, and interpersonal behaviors, such as caretaking, controlling, dependency, poor communication, weak boundaries, lack of trust, anger, and sex problems.

People in helping professions often identify with this list. We are involved in providing care to others. Some of us may have been drawn to the helping professions in the first place because of a feeling of low self-worth.

We often find that control is an issue for us as helpers. For instance, we may believe that we must control people and situations because we cannot trust that the outcome will be satisfactory with less competent involvement. That belief is often reinforced by a client who places complete trust in a professional and who prefers not to make his or her own major decisions. Sometimes the client has always relied on others, or he or she is depressed, fatigued, or overwhelmed by the number and complexity of decisions to be made. The co-dependent professional who is very competent, trustworthy, and has a need to control finds it easy to fall into this trap. It is a trap because self-determination is related to responsibility and positive self-esteem, which are problem areas for virtually all chemically dependent clients and many chronically ill clients.

The co-dependent has an uncanny ability to feel the feelings of another person. A co-dependent professional may also have difficulty differentiating between his or her own feelings and those of the client. For example, when working with a depressed client, a co-dependent helper may internalize the client's feelings and become depressed.

Alcohol Abuse in the Elderly

Alcohol abuse is more prevalent in the elderly than most people, including many helping professionals, realize. Schuckit (1989) notes that

> there is at least preliminary evidence that the rate of severe alcohol impairment among individuals over the age of 50 or over the age of 65 (depending on the specific survey used) is only slightly less than the general population. Thus, between 1% and 3% of women and 5% and 12% of men over the age of 60 are likely to have severe and repetitive alcohol life problems . . . 10% to 20% of older men and women being seen by outreach agencies or who are residing in nursing homes would fulfill alcoholism criteria, as would 20% to 40% . . . seen in psychiatric clinics and 20% to 60% . . . [in] acute medical care. (p. 1)

Alcohol abuse in older persons may be an even greater problem than in young persons. Older adults tend to take more medications and have less physical reserve to help their bodies overcome the negative effects of the mixtures with which they medicate themselves. Further, the alcoholics seen by helping persons in gerontology are probably late-onset alcoholics, because individuals whose alcoholism began at an early age are unlikely to live long enough to become old (Schuckit, 1989).

Parallel Issues of Co-Dependency and Countertransference

STIGMA AND DENIAL

Substance abuse is a disease of denial (Kellerman, 1980; Mueller & Ketcham, 1987). The user denies the abuse or its negative consequences; the co-dependent denies the severity of the problem. Service providers and helping professionals may also collude in denial by overlooking the possibility of alcohol or other drug abuse. This can be especially difficult if the helping professional grew up in an alcoholic family and learned to use denial as a defense mechanism.

Before her work as a social worker in senior housing, Paula often turned down training opportunities about aging and alcoholism. Her colleagues asked her to explain this behavior, atypical for someone who attended every other training event within a 100-mile radius of her work and home, and many that were at a great distance. Her explanation was usually, "There are thousands of people doing alcoholism; I do other things and refer alcohol problems to those who have taken the training."

A few years later, Paula began to attend Al-Anon meetings. She turned to this program, for the family and friends of alcoholics, because she could no longer deny her son's abuse of alcohol and his addiction to other drugs. Later, for the first time, Paula recognized that her former husband was an alcoholic, and finally "remembered" that her father also drank to excess. Paula had resisted exposure to information about addiction because she had to maintain her denial.

Denial was Paula's only defense against the guilt she experienced about her son's substance abuse, and the shame she had internalized in her childhood. When a helping professional is prone to denial in his or her personal life, it will be present in professional life as well. Denial may prevent the service provider and the client from even naming the problem. Once the disease of substance abuse has been diagnosed, naming it becomes the challenge—especially when many older clients are offended by the terms "alcoholic" or "addict."

ANGER

Excessive anger at clients with alcohol or drug problems is another countertransference hook for co-dependent professionals. People who grew up in alcoholic homes may have been abused for expressing their anger. They learn to keep their anger inside, storing it up until it becomes rage (Seixas & Youch, 1985). Their rage may haunt their professional work, as Janet's did.

Janet, an outreach worker, found herself unduly angry, in fact, irrationally so, with some of her clients. She felt anger rise when they called, drunk and crying for help. Wrestling with anger and aware of the futility of making yet another referral to a recovery program, she battled her own need to give her clients the opportunity to just sit with her and talk things over—which worked wonderfully with other clients. Neither referrals nor traditional counseling techniques work while an individual is drinking or using. Anger was the expression of Janet's feelings of inadequacy; she wanted to be a great outreach worker who helped her clients find sobriety.

As a child, Janet had not learned how to be appropriately angry. Raised in an alcoholic home, it was not safe to be angry at her parents. When she expressed anger by word or action, she was verbally or physically reprimanded, often abusively. Her father's brutality and her mother's inability to protect her taught Janet to store her anger inside. When alcoholic and other dependent clients presented themselves to her she responded professionally, as she had been trained to do. She followed the agency's procedures, completed forms, and made an effort to establish trust. She worked hard to get over the feeling that her clients' abilities to get and stay sober were directly related to her ability as a helping professional—that if she were "good enough" the treatment would work.

However, Janet found herself less and less able to cope with her anger. Sometimes she compensated by being more pleasant, more accommodating. Other times she transferred clients to colleagues, admitting that she was too emotionally volatile. Janet found working with clients who triggered her anger to be much more difficult than working with clients who did not. She identified the problem as blaming alcoholic clients for their own problems.

People who are unable to express anger learn to "stuff it" (Beattie, 1987). Janet was pulled between her early childhood training, her clients' needs to be challenged about their self-destructive behaviors, and her own need to express anger—a valid emotion. This was her triangle of countertransference (see Chapter 1).

Then Janet learned to re-channel her anger and use it constructively, for example, in situations where she was needed to advocate on behalf of a client within a bureaucratic system, which she found intimidating or hopelessly complex. When possible, she might wait to confront a difficult physician, Social Security Administration employee, or social service worker until those moments of anger appeared to give her the energy, tenacity, and terse vocabulary to cope with a problem and follow it through the system.

At other times, when she noticed the feelings of extreme irritation at little things, agitation, and inability to focus, she often found intense anger behind it. She could relieve the anger by naming it, by taking a short break from the work at hand, and by examining her triangle of countertransference for cues as to what pushed her anger button.

NEEDING TO BE NEEDED AND OVERHELPING

Helping professionals who grew up in alcoholic families, or who are currently involved with a chemically dependent partner or child, may have earned their place in the sun as children by being extraordinarily responsible (Gravitz & Bowden, 1985). Taking care of and taking over for an alcoholic parent may have been the only way to get their own and other family members' basic needs met. Neighbors and other relatives tend to honor the child who cleans, cooks, and looks after younger children in the family. A helping professional with this background may face countertransference when a substance-abusing client is unable to fulfill his or her responsibilities. The professional's instinct may be to take on that client's responsibilities at the expense of the client's opportunities for independence, freedom, and recovery.

At times it is in the best interests of elders and their families to teach them to provide services for themselves. This is client self-determination. Sometimes simply teaching people how to use the network of services is astonishingly difficult when they have not had any previous experience or interest in doing so, are reluctant to believe they need services, or have little energy for coping with many telephone calls and visits to social service agencies. Many alcoholics prefer to be the center of attention, receiving a great many services, but they are reluctant or unable to manage the many parts of complex service delivery systems. In these cases, helping professionals may make a typical co-dependent decision: "It's so much easier to do it myself!" (Beattie, 1987).

Substance abusers often display other types of dependent behavior. They may be unwilling to manage their own health, finances, professional career, or social relations. Dependent clients may have a history of seeking friends, lovers, co-workers, and professional helpers to provide direction, make decisions, and take charge of their lives. Each dependent requires one or more co-dependents in order to remain dependent. Their search usually leads them to co-dependent people who are willing to assume responsibility for the life of another. Family relationships of dependency and co-dependency become enmeshed and appear unusually strong and bonded. However, one or more family members may be destroyed as a result of these pathological relationships. The substance abuser may succumb to physical deterioration as the result of the use of alcohol and other drugs; co-dependents more often die from suicide. Becoming too enmeshed in a dependent client's life can also be destructive to the co-dependent helping professional.

SELF-CONDEMNATION AND SHAME

The participants in dependent/co-dependent interactions experience some degree of self-condemnation and shame. The abuser tends to blame him- or herself for lack of control over life and lack of control over the substance. When substance abuse has advanced to the stage where denial is no longer possible, the abuser feels great shame, whether intoxicated or sober (Bradshaw, 1988).

Co-dependents also are often ashamed of themselves because of their loved one's substance abuse. They believe that if they were articulate enough, or forceful enough, or intelligent enough, they could solve the problems for the dependent person (Gravitz & Bowden, 1985).

Helping professionals may find themselves in the same situation, believing, "If I were good at my work I could save my client."

Helping professionals also may be ashamed that their clients cannot manage substances, money, emotions, or relationships. They blame themselves for being inadequate to the task.

Self-Righteousness and Blame

The counterparts of self-condemnation and shame are self-righteousness and blame. The underlying thought here is, "I may be bad, but I don't . . ." In a dependent/co-dependent relationship, each participant blames the other for the situation. The user may blame the co-dependent for the substance abuse, even when the abuse started years before the dependent and co-dependent met. Alternately, the co-dependent may blame the abuser for the co-dependent's life situation, saying, "If it weren't for you, I'd . . ." Co-dependents may also blame external events for a dependent person's substance abuse or other behaviors.[1]

When the helping professional recognizes shame as an irrational response to the client's chemical dependency or other dependent behavior, the alternate response may be blame. Blaming the client, the doctor, the system, or any external individual is the reflexive response to irrational shame. It is realistic for a professional to become weary of a client's telephone calls relating that she or he is out of money and in need of groceries at the same time *every* month, in spite of the clear budget the professional helped prepare. A co-dependent professional may think: "If only . . ." If only the client had more money, if only she wouldn't give so much to her son, if only the client would stick to the budget, then the client could make it through the month. If the client is dependent, she may be unable to take these seemingly simple steps on her own behalf. In a wave of self-righteous feelings, the professional knows that she or he would manage differently.

Dependent and co-dependent persons commonly move back and forth between the two poles of shame and blame. The countertransference issue here is the shame/blame trap: If I were a good enough helper, I could make a difference in my chemically dependent client; if it weren't for my client's substance abuse, he or she wouldn't need help (and I could get on to someone who does need help and, incidentally, might be much more appreciative).

The solution to the shame/blame trap is detachment. Detachment does not mean disconnecting from the client. It does mean remaining compassionate while recognizing that sometimes the professional's help will not solve the client's problem, that the client's substance abuse is a problem that the professional did not cause, and that it is not the professional's responsibility.[2]

Clarence came to his alcoholic "bottom" two or three times each year. At this point he would seek help, often from the social worker in his senior housing unit. He would sit at her desk crying about how bad he was and how much he wanted and needed help. At the first of these episodes, Donna, a new social worker, referred Clarence to an outpatient recovery program. He participated in the counseling for a few months, but did not stop drinking. Finally he stopped the counseling. Several times, he appeared in the lobby of his building obviously drunk, but he avoided Donna.

Months later, he contacted Donna again, pleading for help. This time she suggested that he admit himself to a more intensive treatment program nearby that had an immediate opening. In the midst of a major anxiety attack, Clarence begged Donna to go with him. She questioned whether she should. Was accompanying him healthy or was it co-dependent? After "taking" a few minutes to think about it, she agreed to go. She reasoned that alcoholism was a disease and that she had accompanied other clients to hospitals with other illnesses in the past. At his further request, she remained with him for half an hour during the intake interview, then left him with the interviewer to complete the admission process.

Going into detoxification was, for Clarence, like going into physical hell. It would have been easy for Donna at that point to get pulled into Clarence's fear, to reassure him, to tell him everything would be fine. It also would have been easy for Donna to get overinvolved, to become anxious about whether Clarence would drop out of the program, and to believe she could make Clarence get better if only she were a good enough social worker.

Leaving the facility was a conscious act of detachment on Donna's part. She realized that she had done what she could to help Clarence. Following through and giving up alcohol were Clarence's responsibilities, not Donna's.

Her detachment was more successful than the treatment. Clarence appeared in the lobby of his apartment building a few days later; he had not remained in the treatment center. Donna accepted his decision without comment and without falling into either the shame or blame posture.

Months later, when Clarence committed suicide, Donna had to make this effort again. She had to acknowledge that Clarence said no to treatment and yes to suicide, that he was ultimately responsible for his own life. Nothing she could have done would have changed his decisions. Donna came from an alcoholic family herself, and she attended Al-Anon meetings. She used the meetings, her support group, and supervision to work through and accept Clarence's regrettable choice of a solution to his problems and the fact that her help could not always save her alcoholic clients.

OVERIDENTIFICATION WITH FAMILY MEMBERS

Over-identification with family members of substance abusing clients is another area of vulnerability for professionals with similar backgrounds. Like abusers, co-dependents must be given information and then left to act on it on their own.

Laura, a practitioner whose older client was in danger from her alcoholic son, refused to seek help to forcibly remove the "boy"—who was now in his 50s. A few years earlier, Laura had faced a similar issue with her own 18-year-old son. It was a difficult moment for Laura. She knew what needed to be done and had a good idea of how her client felt about this action. Should she disclose her own experience? Or should she join other professionals in forcing their recommendation that the son be removed? Laura finally decided to support the recommendations of others and use her knowledge of the feelings such an act evoked to express her empathy with the client. Another family member was brought in, and the alcoholic son was eventually removed from the household.

LOSS OF BOUNDARIES

Many people who come from substance abusing families grow up without a sense of boundaries. Losing one's boundaries is typical behavior for co-dependent individuals. Even professionally trained helpers who are also co-dependents may find it difficult to continue to think of a client as a client when the client and helper have been together for a long time, have been through several crises, and have shared some of the client's most intimate moments.

Some of us may never have identified our boundaries. The signal that they have been violated may come after the fact. We feel oppressed by a client, overwhelmed by his or her difficulties, and a supervisor may tell us that we have become "over involved." This may be a particular problem with certain older clients who have not had the services of psychotherapists, social workers, home health aides, or other helpers in the past, because family members and trusted friends have taken care of their needs. These clients need to see their professional helpers as friends in order to be comfortable accepting services. The problem may be compounded when services are provided in the client's home, making a professional visit appear more like the visit of a friend.

A friend lives with a very different code of behavior than a helping professional. A friend may not wish to confront an individual with his or her self-destructive behavior; a professional may need to do so. A friend may not be willing to present a client with unpleasant alternatives; a professional may need to do so. A friend may help by performing many and varied tasks, saving an ill individual the problem of trying to relate to several different people. A professional helper may have to teach a family member to provide a service, refer the client to another agency, or contract for the services of another individual, depending on caseload and job description. The client cannot have this "friend" for all services and must face new people, new agencies, and new relationship problems—often when feeling least able to cope. The war between personal history, training, and the client's need to cast a professional helper as a friend requires constant vigilance if boundaries are to remain clear.

Using Countertransference for
Personal and Professional Growth

Recovery is no less essential for the co-dependent than it is for the substance abuser. Without it, co-dependents tend to slip back into old familiar patterns of denial, over-helping, feeling shame or blaming the client when interventions are not successful, becoming heavily invested in the outcomes of interventions, or losing personal boundaries.

Alcoholics Anonymous and Al-Anon can be of great benefit to helping professionals, just as they are for alcohol abusers and their families and friends. Professionals who see co-dependent patterns in their behavior may make remarkable strides in these programs, particularly if they combine them with good supervision on the job. Helping professionals have established meetings just for themselves, where work on both their professional concerns and personal lives can proceed with the assurance that clients will not be attending the same meeting. These professional support groups are highly recommended for reducing stress on the job, clarifying job descriptions, and analyzing boundaries.

UNDERSTANDING COUNTERTRANSFERENCE CUES

One practitioner said that one of the cues of countertransference for her was extraordinary fatigue when working with a particular client or family. Another was feeling that she needed to "pull their arms and legs off of me while I was walking home." This worker walked home because the exercise and time helped her to process the end of the work day. It helped her manage the stress that resulted from her co-dependence and countertransference.

Dorothy Heyman (1989) of the Women's (Alcoholism) Program, North of Market Senior Services in San Francisco, says about working with alcoholic clients, "If you feel helpless, if you feel inadequate, join the club!" There are many special problems, she notes, including misdiagnosis or the disease not being diagnosed at all. Doctors often have not received enough training in alcoholism and they are affected by society's belief that alcoholism is not a problem for older adults, particularly older women.

Heyman (1989) makes these recommendations for helping professionals working with alcoholic clients:

- Know your own "slippery places," and avoid them.
- Be alert for symptoms of burnout and frustration.
- Admit that what you are doing is hard.
- Have reasonable expectations.
- Nurture yourself.
- Set limits; needy people tend to be more demanding.
- Find a healthy way to get your own needs met.
- Accept clients where they are—see the person behind the bottle.
- If you are in over your head, let your client know.

Self-monitoring is an important tool. The following are some questions helpers might ask themselves to help determine if they have fallen into countertransference and co-dependency traps:

Do you seek guidance, feedback, and assistance from other professionals to keep from getting hooked into unhealthy behaviors with alcoholic or addicted clients? Professionals from the chemical dependency field are excellent resources for getting help for ourselves.

Do you communicate clearly with alcoholic clients? Direct communication about the client's drinking problem is essential to let him or her know that you know. Many chemically dependent individuals believe that they are able to hide their substance abuse and that if anyone knew, that person would no longer work with the abuser. By denying the problem of substance abuse, you reinforce these mistaken beliefs. By being direct and maintaining the helping connection, you refute them.

Do you assist clients to realize, feel, know, be aware of, and be responsible for the consequences of their drinking behavior or drug use? Professionals in denial sometimes unwittingly go along with the alcoholic client whose recent fall was blamed on the chore worker who put a piece of furniture in the wrong place, or on another external event. Often the truth is: If the client had not been drunk, it would have been possible to avoid the piece of furniture.

Do you let the alcoholic or addict take care of his or her needs? Or, if the client can no longer do that, are you direct in addressing the problem and do you make appropriate arrangements? Alcoholism or alcoholic dementia does not get better without treatment; clients who have deteriorated to the point of needing help will always need it. Therefore, the situation must be faced with appropriate resources.

Do you limit services because the person is drunk, as the hospital team did in Chapter 3? Are you slow to admit alcoholic people for services and quick to discharge them? This, too, may be a sign of denial.

Do you let the alcoholic or addict clear up his or her own mistakes? One of the ways co-dependent behavior in families manifests itself is in the way family members cover the mistakes of the substance abuser. A helper may be accustomed to handling hassles with the telephone company for older clients. With an alcoholic client, stepping in to solve the problem may be co-dependent behavior, keeping the client from facing the consequences of chemical dependency.

Do you express concern to the alcoholic or addict about his or her behavior, especially in relationship to alcohol or other drugs? The diseases of alcoholism or drug addiction are fatal; helpers are appropriately concerned.

Are you careful not to make threats that you won't carry out? Threatening the client with the loss of service if she is not compliant has no impact unless there is intention to follow that plan. Alcoholics in recovery have often said of the co-dependents in their lives, "I didn't hear the words, I watched her feet. She said she'd leave, but I knew she wouldn't do it."

Do you point out the alcoholic's or the addict's inappropriate behavior? Any inappropriate behavior is a clue to the client's condition, and pointing it out to them is another way through the denial that keeps them from sobriety.[3]

THE POSITIVE SIDE OF CO-DEPENDENCE

While I have emphasized the negatives of co-dependency here, both co-dependence and countertransference also have positive sides. Both help professionals to develop empathy with client needs—sometimes before the client is able to articulate those needs. One client described her social worker as someone who "gives me what I need before I know I need it!" It is no wonder that co-dependents are sought out as helpers. A co-dependent professional who is informed and aware of the possibility and symptoms of inappropriate helping is able to provide "healthier" help—healthier for both client and professional.

Summary

Helping professionals who work with alcoholic older clients may fall into a set of unhealthy behaviors called co-dependency, particularly if they have had a substance-abusing family member. Some of these behaviors that arise in service to the elderly include denial, inappropriate anger, overhelping, shame, blame, overidentification with family members, and loss of personal boundaries. When helping professionals become aware of these problems, consultation, in-service training, professional support groups, Alcoholics Anonymous and Al-Anon programs, plus good professional supervision, can be of great help. Working with alcoholic clients can lead professionals to feel helpless, but unhooking from co-dependent behavior can lead to a healthier situation for both client and professional.

Notes

1. This information provided by Cottage Meeting Programs: Information and Education about Alcoholism and Co-Dependency; 1823 Ninth Street; Berkeley, CA 94710.

2. For additional information on detachment, refer to Al-Anon Family Group Headquarters, Inc.; P.O. Box 862; Midtown Station; New York, NY 10018-0862. (*Al-Anon Speaks Out* is an annual newsletter for professionals. The information on "detachment" is from that literature; it is also published separately as a brochure titled *Detachment*, Conference Approved Literature S-19, which is available at Al-Anon Family Group meetings.)

3. This list of questions was adapted from a list provided by the National Council on Alcoholism (NCOA), Bay Area. There are offices of the NCOA throughout the United States, which are staffed by trained paid and volunteer staff.

References

Beattie, M. (1987). *Co-Dependent no more*. New York: Harper & Row.
Bradshaw, J. (1988). *Healing the shame that binds you*. Deerfield Beach, FL: Health Communications.

Gravitz, H. L., & Bowden, J. D. (1985). *Guide to recovery: A book for adult children of alcoholics.* Holmes Beach, FL: Learning Publications.

Heyman, D. (1989, August). Alcoholism and the elderly. Inservice training conducted at Women's Alcoholism Project, North of Market Senior Alcoholism Program, San Francisco, CA.

Kellerman, J. L. (1980). *Alcoholism: A merry-go-round named denial.* Center City, MN: Hazelden Educational Materials.

Mueller, L. A., & Ketcham, K. (1987). *Recovering, how to get and stay sober.* New York: Bantam Books.

Schaef, A. W. (1986). *Co-Dependence: Misunderstood-mistreated.* San Francisco: Harper & Row.

Schuckit, M. A. (1989). Alcohol, drugs, and the elderly. *Drug Abuse & Alcoholism Newsletter, 3.*

Seixas, J. S., & Youch, G. (1985). *Children of alcoholism: A survivor's manual.* New York: Perennial Library/Harper & Row.

8

Recognizing Countertransference: A Key to Good Nursing Home Placement

MARTHA SEBASTIAN-MOYER

The working relationship between helping professionals and individuals and families considering nursing home placement can be very emotionally charged and complex. Placing a loved one in a nursing home can evoke familial guilt, anger, and resentment. The family member being placed may also feel helpless, abandoned, and rejected (Brody, 1977). These intense emotions often activate strong countertransference feelings in helping professionals, who may be dealing with similar issues themselves. Very little emphasis is placed on this area in current professional and lay literature, or in professional training and supervision. Too often, the result is ineffectual and insensitive professional intervention with individuals and families making this painful, important decision.

Negative Stereotypes of Nursing Homes

In our culture, nursing homes and other long-term care facilities have negative reputations. Part of this "poor press" is based on reality. The average nursing home costs between $2,000 and $3,000 per month. Without comprehensive national health insurance for long-term care, the elderly must finance nursing home stays with their own funds, typically until they spend down to the poverty level. At-home spouses are now required to spend all of the couple's assets down to somewhere between $12,000 and $60,000, depending on the state. This financial reality casts a pall over the helping professional, as well as over the individual and family considering nursing home placement. Nursing homes often take the rap for our nation's lack of social planning and public responsibility.

Another reality is that conditions in some nursing homes are very bad for both staff and patients. Most physical care and patient supervision is provided by aides who are poorly paid and poorly trained and who are forced to work long hours under demoralizing conditions. Frequently from different economic and social classes than the patients they care for, these employees are often the focus of anger for both patients and families. Aides often receive no inservice training, emotional support, or assistance in coping with the issues of physical decline, death, and loss that they encounter each day. Their unacknowledged and unresolved countertransference feelings can lead them to protect themselves from facing these issues by depersonalizing or infantilizing the older patient, for example, "come and eat your food, honey." They may also take out their anger and frustration at the system in which they work and the society in which they live by stealing from patients. Or they may leave patients in their urine or feces longer than they need to, or tie them into a wheelchair to sit in the hallway and stare into space. Families often blame the poor care their loved ones receive in a nursing home on the poor caliber of staff. Unresolved staff countertransference issues may be equally to blame for poor patient care and high staff turnover.

John, age 23, a black father of two children, had to take two buses to get to his job as a nurse's aide on the night shift of a nursing home. Usually a responsible and caring employee,

John was very impatient and rough when he handled Marion. Marion was 75, wealthy, demanding and had Alzheimer's disease. Marion's roommate finally told the head nurse about John's rough treatment. When confronted by the nurse, John initially denied that he was in error. Later, he agreed to attend a seminar I gave on countertransference for nursing home employees in his city.

In the seminar, John drew a three generational diagram called a genogram. It showed members of his family and provided a springboard for looking at events and people in his own life who might unwittingly have caused his countertransference problems with Marion. John discovered that Marion, who was white, reminded him of Mrs. Barrington, a very self-centered, wealthy woman who had employed John's mother as a live-in domestic worker for many years. Mrs. Barrington was very demanding and rarely gave John's mother time off to be with her own children. John's rough treatment of Marion was really a result of his long pent-up rage toward Mrs. Barrington, who had deprived him of his own mother, and toward a prejudiced world that kept both John and his mother in low-paying positions of servitude.

By the end of the seminar, John had resolved to vastly improve his treatment of Marion. He also decided to turn his anger into energy to help him change his life situation. My follow-up contacts with John revealed that he returned to school on a part-time basis and is now a registered nurse in a major city hospital.

When helping professionals recommend against nursing home placement because they generalize that there aren't "any decent ones out there," they eliminate the need to deal with their own countertransference issues of aging, disability, abandonment, and guilt, which are so often brought to the surface by the dynamics of a nursing home placement. This often prevents patients from getting the socialization and physical care they need, and families from getting relief from their excessive stress (Brody, 1977). Smith and Bengtston (1979) have reported that, when relieved of the stress of caring for an older relative, the closeness of relationships within families is continued, renewed, or even newly discovered in the nursing home.

Helping Professional as
Surrogate Family Member

Professionals and clients often become emotional members of each others' families. According to gerontologist Bonnie Genevay, the roles of the professional and client are not always based on their respective chronological ages. Genevay has sometimes been seen by older clients, especially those with cognitive dysfunction, as being their mother even though she was closer in age to their adult children. At other times, she has been seen as their surrogate daughter when her age was close to the client's.

Case managers (see Chapter 10) are particularly vulnerable to overstepping their surrogate family member roles. Older people who require case management are often isolated, without a family support system, physically fragile, and/or cognitively impaired. They are often a step away from a nursing home. A high percentage of nursing home residents are widowed, unmarried, childless, or have only one adult child (Brody, 1977). Case managers, by definition, must be able to move into some aspects of their clients' lives and partially take over. Since most client contact is made in the home, it is often easy for helping professionals to become over-responsible for, and too involved with, their clients. Helping professionals who were trained for this role by their personal family dynamics are especially vulnerable to developing counter-transference problems in this area, as did Angie.

Angie, age 29, a professional case manager, had built a close relationship with Marie, age 79, a childless widow. For the two years they had worked together, Angie had helped Marie stay in her own home despite two operations and a stroke. Marie became so frail that she began to fall constantly. She exhibited stroke-related problems with short term memory which necessitated 24-hour supervision. Her physician recommended nursing home placement. Marie adamantly refused placement and implored Angie to help her stay in her own home. Angie began to have headaches and nightmares; she worked overtime to gather more services for Marie without success. Two weeks later Marie fell, broke her hip, and was placed in a nursing home after an acute hospitalization.

Had Angie received adequate supervision, she might have recognized that her unresolved countertransference issues prevented her from accurately assessing Marie's unsafe living situation. Angie had come to depend on the emotional gratification and compliments she received during her frequent visits with Marie in her home. These visits compensated for the emotional cutoff she experienced with her own mother, a wealthy, narcissistic business woman who disapproved of Angie and her work, and who traveled constantly. Although Angie's relationship with Marie temporarily provided her with a mother figure who loved and needed her, it prevented her from dealing with her problems with her own mother.

Marie's placement re-exposed Angie to the feelings of pain, abandonment, and loss she had experienced in her relationship with her absent mother. Fighting Marie's placement prevented Angie from being able to help Marie recognize and work through her terror of leaving her own home and confronting the reality of her own mortality.

The Helping Professional as "Good Adult Child"

The helping professional must be able to understand that each family caregiver has a different ability to tolerate caregiving stress. According to Zarit, Reever, and Bach-Peterson (1980), some caregivers report feeling very high levels of stress even when the patient has very few behavioral changes. Others cope with the most severe changes but report little stress. The severity of behavioral and cognitive symptoms generally has not been found to be a good indicator of caregivers' perception of stress.

If they are not in touch with their own unresolved countertransference issues helping professionals, who are currently long-term caregivers for older spouses or parents at home, may find it hard to understand why their clients choose to place their loved ones in nursing homes rather than continue to care for them at home. Usually exhausted and guilt-ridden, family caregivers are very vulnerable to subtle and not-so-subtle professional feedback that they could "try a little harder." Helping professionals sometimes overlook the fact that each family situation is unique. The client's family may be quite different from the professional's.

When I lead support or therapy groups for adult children who are caring for their aging parents, I am aware that many adult children are still very intimidated by their parents. If and when the time comes to consider placing their parents in a nursing home, they are often too overwhelmed by their guilt and anxiety to go against their parents' wish to stay in their own or their child's home. If the adult child is also a helping professional, he or she may have to work hard to keep from taking out the guilt on clients.

Alice, a middle-aged social worker, had her life turned upside down when her mother, a widow, had a stroke and could no longer live by herself. Alice, a widow herself with a new professional career and college debts to pay off, sacrificed her private life and strained her personal finances to take her mother into her home after she was released from the hospital.

Becoming a caregiver was very stressful for Alice. Fortunately, she was able to utilize her own supervision at work to deal with her strong personal feelings. In supervision, Alice looked at her love for her mother and her resentment and anger about this unexpected continuation of a lifelong pattern of being the responsible child in her family. She also gained support for her desire and need to regain her independence and for her right to get on with her own life, unencumbered by the 24-hour needs of her mother.

After seven months, her mother was well enough to be placed in a nearby retirement home in which personal care and medication supervision was available. Although Alice's guilt was great, and her mother complained nightly, Alice persisted and made the placement. After a rough adjustment period, her mother did very well in the new setting.

Alice might have become very self-righteous in working with other adult caregivers who were placing their parents in institutions without first making the same sacrifices she had made. But Alice was well trained and had good insight. She received supervision that stressed identifying, understanding, and using her countertransference feelings constructively. As a result of this positive countertransference, she was able to enhance her work with family caregivers. Her personal experience with caregiving and the process of deciding to place her mother in the retirement home enabled Alice to quickly pick up on family caregivers' personal stress and feelings of anger and guilt. She found she could help adult children identify and work through their terror of watching their parents' sudden or gradual deterioration. She could also help them cope with the realization that they, too, might be as dependent and vulnerable as their own parents some day.

When Burnout Impedes
Effective Placement Counseling

As a family nears the time when they must place a loved one in a nursing home, they often seek help in handling their feelings of ambivalence, anger, guilt, and grief. If the professionals helping them feel overwhelmed by similar problems in their own lives, it may be too painful for the professionals to allow family members to deal with these feelings in their presence.

Marta, age 44, worked in a senior citizen program that provided counseling and respite for caregivers. She was assigned to work with Rita, age 55. Rita had spent years caring for her 79-year-old husband, Robert, who was suffering from advanced Alzheimer's disease.

When Rita began to call Marta daily with complaints and fears about her own emotional and physical health, Marta suggested that she place Robert in a nursing home but did not encourage Rita to acknowledge or work through her ambivalence about the situation. Rita subsequently placed Robert in a nearby nursing home one day and, overcome by guilt and anxiety, took him home the next day. When Marta heard about this, she became frustrated and angry at Rita.

Realizing that something was amiss, Marta was able to recognize that her reactions to this family necessitated looking at possible countertransference issues in her personal and professional life. She admitted to herself that she was emotionally and physically exhausted, both at home and at work. As the primary source of emotional support for her two teenage children and her nonverbal husband, she was being bombarded daily at work with cries for help from overwhelmed caregivers. She literally did not, and could not, hear Rita's cries for help because they were too close to her own sense of desperation. She had nothing left to give to her clients or her family. She was shutting down professionally, and just going through the motions both at work and at home. Marta also painfully admitted that by encouraging Rita to place Robert prematurely she was trying to get Rita to do what she wasn't doing—unloading caregiving responsibility.

After some thought, Marta made strategic moves within her own family to lighten her emotional load. She successfully involved her husband more with the children's needs, and insisted that she and her husband get marital counseling.

Marta also helped her staff and herself to feel less overwhelmed and responsible for the immense unmet needs of her program's clients. She did this by scheduling a staff retreat where they were able to take a step back from their work and recognize their many accomplishments with and on behalf of clients. The staff also acknowledged that their source of funds was not giving them adequate staffing or respite funding to begin to meet the needs of their assigned population. Their clients, unfortunately, had been told that the program would meet all of their needs. This is the "Earth-Mother" identity that agencies too frequently foster in their marketing to clients—an organizational countertransference issue. The staff was caught between their clients' unrealistic expectations, limited staff and funds, and their own unrealistic desire to do "all things for all people all of the time." Before the retreat, staff were well on their way to burnout. As they worked together to unload their own feelings of overresponsibility for program goals they could not meet, the staff found that both the quality of their work and their job satisfaction vastly improved.

After the retreat, Marta was able to help Rita explore her own fears about what life would be like without her husband, the authority figure in their marriage. The more Marta allowed herself to experience the pain in her own life, and to feel more in control of her personal and professional circumstances, the more she was able to help Rita gain control over her life.

Getting Caught in Families'
Relationship Triangles

Professionals must work hard to avoid getting caught in relationship triangles in families experiencing the conflict of nursing home placement. Family systems theorists and practitioners have long used the concept of relationship triangles to explain how family members organize their relationships with each other. Murray Bowen (1976), one of the fathers of family systems therapy, has described the relationship triangle as "a three person emotional configuration . . . the molecule or basic building block of any emotional system, whether it is in the family or any other group" (p. 75). Bowen observed that "when tensions are very high in families and available family triangles are exhausted, the family system 'triangles in' people from outside the family such as . . . police and social agencies" (p. 75). It is very important for helping professionals to resist allowing triangles in their own family relationships from pulling them into triangles within client families.

The stress of placing a family member in a nursing home can shake a family system to its roots. The issues are many. Money, for example, is a major source of family conflict. One of the adult children, sometimes the exhausted caregiver, may want to encourage the ill parent to spend his or her estate on nursing home care. Another sibling might be counting on parental inheritance to pay bills or buy a home, and may fight the placement.

I have found that bitter and often long-standing sibling rivalries are often at the bottom of financial and other planning problems. The question of who becomes the hands-on or supervisory caregiver among the adult children often reveals a lot about family dynamics. Sometimes it is the overly responsible adult child who continues to fulfill the role. When this caregiver becomes exhausted and can no longer care for the parent, advice and opposition can come from siblings who have made no effort to help out earlier. The family's emotionally and often geographically distant sibling may challenge the caregiver's decision to place the parent in a nursing home, trying to become the expert on what should be done and creating a power struggle within the triangle.

Such dynamics can hook the helping professional in a number of ways. Often, the professional has been the overresponsible sibling in his or her own family. She or he may then overidentify with the super-responsible sibling caregiver and dismiss as unimportant or self-serving the objections raised by the seemingly less-responsible family members. If the helping professional has had the role of being the less-responsible member in his or her own family, he or she might "act out" with the siblings who are against nursing home placement.

Jack, a counselor in a family service agency, worked with a very conflicted family, the Smiths, regarding whether or not Ted Smith, age 55, should place his wife Sue, age 65, in a nursing home against her wishes. Ted was exhausted from 10 years of caring for Sue, who had advanced Parkinson's disease and needed total bed care. Despite all of his efforts to the contrary, Jack found himself siding with the Smith's son, Jeffrey, who was against the placement.

Jack denied the validity of Mr. Smith's claims that he was too exhausted to continue to care for his wife. He avoided meeting with Mr. Smith and resisted including Mrs. Smith in any of the planning. Concerned about this, Jack's supervisor had him explore some of the parallel relationship triangles in his own life. With this encouragement, Jack rediscovered feelings of rage he had felt towards his own father. Five years before his father had placed his mother in a nursing home after she suffered a massive stroke, then divorced her and married another woman. Jack fought the placement and divorce and lost. His mother died shortly thereafter. With his supervisor's help, Jack was able to better understand his strong reactions to the Smith family. Ted Smith was, in fact, not like Jack's father and Ted had good reason to make this nursing home placement. Realizing this, Jack became more helpful to the entire family, especially Mrs. Smith, who had reminded him too much of his own mother.

Helping Professional as "God"

When helping professionals display prejudicial and arrogant behaviors towards the elderly and their families who are considering a nursing home placement, they may, in fact, be caught up in their own unresolved countertransference issues. This is especially true for physicians, whose professional training and status have given them positions of control and authority in this country's health care system. Unless medical students specialize in geriatrics, they are rarely asked to look at ageism and their own countertransference issues in working with the elderly. Most medical schools continue to offer no more than one or two classes on geriatrics to the general practitioners in medicine who continue to treat most of our nation's elderly. Yet, the elderly constitute an increasingly large percentage of the average doctor's patient load. As the baby boomers themselves age, this percentage will vastly increase.

Members of the medical profession, trained to cure, have their own problems when they are confronted by the reality of their patients'—and ultimately their own—mortality.

Sam Brown, M.D., age 32, was highly regarded by the younger patients in his medical group, but older patients and their families had learned to avoid the days he was covering for the practice. Although they respected his competence, they did not feel that he understood or was sensitive to their needs.

Anna, age 79, and her husband Simon, an 82-year-old stroke victim, moved into town to live with their daughter when Anna could no longer care for Simon. They made an appointment to see Dr. Brown. After examining Simon, Dr. Brown insisted that Anna place Simon in a nursing home because of his need for extensive care. Anna politely refused, saying that she and her daughter wanted to keep him home with the family as long as they could take good care of him. This scene was repeated during the next three office visits. When Anna refused again, Dr. Brown exploded. He said that *he* was the doctor and, if she knew what was good for her, she would do what he told her to do.

Dr. Brown's unresolved countertransference issues centered on problems with his parents, who had been quite controlling all of his life. He had partially compensated for his feelings of powerlessness by becoming a doctor. In this role, he could turn the tables on the parental figures who were his patients by being very authoritarian with them. He tended to push nursing home placement because, as an only child, he was scared and threatened by his potential responsibilities should both of his parents become disabled and need his help in order to remain home.

Implications for Practice

All of the professionals in the preceding case examples were well-meaning people who were emotionally vulnerable and influenced by their own issues of aging and dying as well as the family dynamics posed by problems of nursing home placement. Constructive ways to deal with these personal-professional problems include:

1. Avoid burnout, caused by unacknowledged personal and workplace countertransference issues, by utilizing supervision, consultation, support groups, training, and staff retreats.
2. Be aware of when you are playing the role of the "good child" as you work with elderly clients and families.
3. Be aware of when you and your clients are becoming emotional members of each others' families.
4. Provide the best possible working conditions for nursing home staff, including respect, good inservice training, and support.
5. Assume that a nursing home placement may be in the best interest of clients and families until you have proven otherwise.
6. Avoid giving too much of yourself to your job. Part of being a responsible helping professional is to monitor excessive caregiving either at home or at work.
7. Be knowledgeable about your own family hooks—especially the unresolved triangle relationships—and avoid getting pulled into your clients' relationship triangles.
8. Use the power and authority of your chosen profession to enable clients and families to make their own choices and wield their own power. Determine to resolve your countertransference issues rather than saddle your clients and patients with them.

Summary

Countertransference problems can occur between the helping professional and an individual or family considering nursing home placement. The decision is difficult, partly because the negative stereotypes about nursing homes are often true. Helping professionals involved in this decision face several common situations in which countertransference can arise. These include becoming too involved as a surrogate family member, playing the good adult child, burning out, getting caught in family relationship triangles, and "playing God."

Professional training, literature, and ongoing supervision must place more emphasis on the importance of helping professionals being able to identify, understand, and make effective use of countertransference issues in their work. Older people and their families deserve to have the best possible professional interventions as they struggle to make decisions about placing their loved ones in nursing homes and long-term care facilities.

References

Bowen, M. (1976). Theory in the practice of psychotherapy. In P. Guerin (Ed.), *Family therapy: Theory and practice.* New York: Gardner Press.

Brody, E. (1977). *Long term care of older people: A practical guide.* New York: Human Services Press.

Smith, K., & Bengtston, V. (1979). Positive consequences of institutionalization: Solidarity between elderly parents and their middle age children. *The Gerontologist, 19,* pp. 438-447.

Zarit, S., Reever, K., & Bach-Peterson, J. (1980). Relatives of the impaired elderly: Correlates of feelings of burden. *The Gerontologist, 20,* pp. 649-655.

9

Sharing Despair:
Working with Distressed Caregivers

SUSAN DELMAESTRO

It is difficult to work with people who are handling a major life challenge and facing the gradual decline of a significant loved one. We are likely to experience in our work much of what the caregiver experiences at home, the continuing struggle to help someone live with dignity and to feel our efforts are worthwhile even when change is slow or nonexistent. Yet, this link between us as professional helpers, and caregivers as family helpers, can provide a rich

AUTHOR'S NOTE: The author wishes to thank Renée Katz, Bonnie Genevay, Dolores Gallagher Thompson, Larry Thompson, Vincent Gong, and Jon Rose for their invaluable help. This work was supported in part by Grant No. AG04572 from the National Institute of Aging.

source from which compassion and the seeds for the therapeutic connection can be drawn.

As professional helpers, we often experience an emotional connection to our clients. We identify with them, their plight, their steps forward, and their steps backward. Both professional caregivers and family caregivers have chosen to be helpers; both see duty and commitment to others as an important part of who they are. In working with our clients, we, in essence, work with reflections of ourselves.

Identifying with Caregivers

As professional helpers, we are likely to respect family caregivers' loyalty, devotion, self-sacrifice, and persistence in the face of adversity. While this helps increase our empathy with clients, it can also hinder our work. Our identification with caregivers can decrease our professional objectivity and judgment (Rose & Del-Maestro, 1990). For instance, we may not see the needs and the fears that underlie some of their self-sacrifice. We may feel threatened by the realization that we, too, could lose those closest to us. Our fears may cause us to defend our client's neediness when our focus should, in fact, be to explore and understand it. Our loneliness may cause us to unduly protect our clients from facing their own eventual aloneness.

To illustrate, I offer the following clinical example:

I held individual counseling sessions with Barbara, a 49-year-old woman who cared for Danny, her 52-year-old husband who suffered from an advanced stage of Alzheimer's disease. Barbara was very depressed about her home situation, yet she did not wish to place Danny in a nursing home or even to make use of respite or in-home help services. I wondered, on the one hand, why Barbara could not let go of Danny and face how far he had deteriorated. Yet, I also found myself allowing her to stray from this issue in sessions, and even defending her self-sacrificing approach to myself. I easily identified with Barbara's loyalty to Danny, with whom she had shared so many years of her life. It wasn't until sometime later in our work, however, that I realized how much I was also threatened by my identification with Barbara, threatened by the thought that I, too, could lose the person I most love. Many difficult sessions followed in which I struggled, trying not to collude with Barbara's denial of her fears. Until I was able to recognize my own fears, I was not able to bring Barbara to look at hers. Having Barbara talk about the loss she was facing was not an easy task, and I was never fully successful. Yet, I was able to mention her loss, to say I could understand how frightening it might be, and to say I thought she would survive it. Before the end of our work, I was able to plant some seeds that would be there for her when she was ready.

Identifying with our caregiver clients may take many forms. As members of families, working with caregivers draws us to re-evaluate our commitment to our own loved ones. We are brought face to face with our feelings about assuming care for another. We may look at our relationships with parents, spouses, and significant others. We may try to determine our own willingness to undertake their care if they should suffer from disease or injury. We may even feel guilty because we do not want to provide care. Awareness of our feelings can lead us to establish new limits in old relationships, to find more comfortable levels of commitment to those we care about. Our willingness to be caregivers is, in addition, likely to directly impact our therapeutic work. For instance, how might a personal decision to place an elderly father in a nursing home affect a helper's attitude toward someone who cares for his or her parent at home? How do our feelings about caring for a husband who has Parkinson's disease influence how we see someone who decides not to take on the care of his or her spouse? It is essential for us to become aware of our own thoughts, feelings, and values—as individuals, as adult children of our parents, and as spouses. It becomes imperative that we understand how these feelings influence us as helpers.

In my work as a therapist with caregivers, several issues continually come to the forefront. These issues are common to caregiving. They are a natural part of caring for a loved one with whom you are slowly losing touch. Experiencing powerlessness, hopelessness, anger, and despair, or denying that a loved one is ill, all can be part of the process of caregiving. These experiences, in addition, can be very much a part of our own processes as we work with caregivers.

Powerlessness

THE FAMILY CAREGIVER'S EXPERIENCE

When caregivers are faced with the reality that their loved ones are not improving and, in fact, may even be worsening, they are likely to feel powerless. They may compensate for their sense of powerlessness by personalizing the downhill course of their loved one's illness. They may see themselves as responsible for their loved one's physical and emotional well-being. To cope with feeling helpless, caregivers may direct their energies into being better caregivers with the hope that they will beat the illness, and, in turn, beat their feelings of distress. Some caregivers make financial sacrifices to afford expensive experimental treatments; others leave satisfying employment to work with their loved ones on a full-time basis. One caregiver I know of played word games every evening with her husband who had Alzheimer's disease. When she could no longer do this because of work commitments and a general sense of fatigue, she blamed herself for her husband's increasing cognitive decline. All of these caregivers feel powerless in their struggle to hold onto their loved ones and compensate by telling themselves that they have the ability to save them.

THE HELPER'S EXPERIENCE

Many countertransference reactions may arise when working with caregivers struggling to maintain control in an uncontrollable situation. We have no easy cures, no magic solutions to share, and we are thus reminded of our own limitations. We may react by becoming overinvolved in the progress of our clients, and we, too, may find ourselves feeling as if we have failed when our clients continue to appear distressed. Forced to grapple with our own powerlessness, we may feel a strong pull to side with the caregiver's struggle to "fix" their loved one. We may find ourselves giving advice, seeking services, or offering assistance beyond the boundaries of the services we provide because we feel desperate and out-of-control when we can't fix a caregiver. For example, as helping professionals, we are in a position to offer caregivers alternative types of care. If we feel powerless, we may find ourselves introducing, and even encouraging, the option of nursing home placement for a loved one. While placement is a viable and often appropriate option, we may also lean toward it because this intervention gives our client an immediate sense of relief, and, thus, in a sense, relieves us of our own feelings of impotency.

Conversely, we may attempt to "unload" the client in order to avoid facing our impotent feelings. We might tell ourselves, for instance, that the caregiver needs a different form of intervention or a special expertise that we cannot offer. We may decide a client is too resistant at this time and is not in a position to be helped. We may suggest, for example, some simple behavioral interventions for a caregiver to use with their loved one. If the caregiver fails to use our suggestions, we may see him or her as unmotivated to improve his or her living situation or resistant—and as a result close the case and hand him or her a list of referrals. In effect, we dismiss a client's request for help. By taking this black-and-white approach, we are really trying to avoid feeling inadequate and helpless. We can decide to shut down these feelings, or we can choose to use them. If we can remember that our client, too, is most likely feeling inadequate and helpless, then we can potentially find common ground, a foundation for our work. Most caregivers I have worked with have benefited much more from knowing that a professional understood their feelings of helplessness and despair, than from being given a quick and easy solution.

Denial

THE FAMILY CAREGIVER'S EXPERIENCE

While many caregivers intellectually accept the illness of their loved one, they may continue to act in ways that deny this reality. This is especially true if their life situation does not match their earlier expectations, which is common since few of us are prepared, at any age, to care for a dependent loved one. A 55-year-old woman, for example, who expects to start thinking about retirement with her husband instead is faced with thinking about nursing home placement for him as his Parkinson's disease worsens. A 30-year-old mother of two preschool-age children wants to put her energies into her growing family, but instead spends much of her time with her mother, who has Alzheimer's disease. Rather than face the situation and all of its implications for her children, her husband, and herself, she may simply deny the illness and its impact. Unfinished business also may contribute to caregiver denial.

Sally has been in a conflictual marriage with Joe for 35 years. She has felt unappreciated by Joe since the early years of their marriage, and now, when Joe has suffered a severe stroke, she senses that her time with him is running short. She wants to finally feel appreciated by Joe for being a good wife. She runs herself ragged as a caregiver trying to do more to please him. She refuses any help from family or friends because that would mean giving up opportunities in which Joe might recognize all she's done for him. Sally does not feel ready to let Joe go since the unfinished business of her marriage, her need to be recognized and appreciated as a wife, remains. Sally needs to deny to herself that Joe is impaired and that, at this late stage, all of her work is unlikely to bring any appreciation.

THE HELPER'S EXPERIENCE

As helpers, we are susceptible to our own personal challenges when we work with caregiver denial. On one level, we may be aware that underlying denial is the reason for a caregiver's inability to accept the loss of a loved one. Yet, we may collude with the client to deny the loss if this taps into our own need to deny grief, and our own fear of loss and abandonment. We may have lived through losses in our lives that we have never fully resolved and have loved ones to whom we have never really said our final goodbyes. In our need to ward off emotional pain, we may direct clients away from experiencing their sense of loss and aloneness. We may feel afraid of facing life without our parent, or our spouse or partner, and protect ourselves by supporting our client's denial of the loss of his or her parent or spouse. If we have not come to terms with illnesses in our own family, we may even deny to ourselves that our client's loved one is seriously ill. Ultimately, facing the decline of another human being shakes our belief in our own immortality. It is this personal challenge—facing our own death—that brings us to our greatest struggle with denial.

Despair

THE FAMILY CAREGIVER'S EXPERIENCE

A common experience for many caregivers is feeling hopeless and trapped (Gallagher, Wrabetz, Lovett, DelMaestro, & Rose, 1989; Gallagher, Rose, Rivera, Lovett, & Thompson, in press). Frustration and demoralization can come easily to a person faced with years of caring for a loved one. At times, hopelessness, the feeling that there are no options or relief, can lead to such great despair that elder abuse occurs. Elder abuse occurs in a small number of cases and is not representative of the actions of the majority of caregivers. But it is important to understand, because it is a sign of the total despair that can result from the tremendous stress that caregivers withstand. It is important to look at the dynamics of elder abuse because, when we work with clients who abuse their loved ones, our feelings toward our clients and our work are powerfully affected.

Caregivers who resort to physical abuse to alter their distressing situations are often desperate and hopeless. They may see themselves as having failed as caregivers. Although they may seek the help of a professional, they may feel so hopeless that no amount of help is sufficient. These caregivers are likely to feel isolated in their lives and disconnected in treatment. They may continue, though, to get professional help because it is their last hope. They may allow the practitioner to see the signs of their desperation, but may still feel overwhelmed because no therapeutic intervention can meet their extreme need. Eventually, they come to feel that nothing is changing or will ever change for them. They may even come to see physical abuse as the only way to have an impact on their loved one and communicate the full extent of their frustration and pain.

THE HELPER'S EXPERIENCE

As helpers, we may have a long history of working with the caregiver prior to the abusive act. Thus, we may be especially prone to have strong feelings of frustration and failure because we have been unable to prevent abuse. We are likely to feel impotent, frustrated, angry, and betrayed by our client. We may feel slapped in the face by the client who has not responded to our hard work and professional advice. To ward off a sense of our own failure, we may not recognize or report the abusive incident. We may tell ourselves that we can find the right intervention to prevent further abuse. We may put ourselves under unnecessary strain by not reporting the abuse and even suffer ethical and legal ramifications because we are required by law to report any suspicion of physical abuse to the appropriate agency. Thus it is important for us to consult with our colleagues when we suspect abuse, since our judgement about reporting is likely to be clouded.

Reporting abuse and accepting that we have not worked miracles with our client may bring us to our own sense of despair about the therapeutic relationship. We may feel angry, betrayed, misunderstood, and unable to work any longer with the abusive caregiver. We may experience the same sense of hopelessness that the caregiver has expressed. While we may initially respond to the client with a tone of efficiency and urgency, our feelings of inadequacy and guilt may prevent us from forming a deeper connection with the client and his or her pain. We may have difficulty facing our task at this time, which is to move beyond our guilt and rebuild the working alliance.

> I worked for several months with Nancy, a 52-year-old woman caring for her husband of 26 years. We spent our time together trying to understand why Nancy couldn't feel any relief. I did not want to see the extent of Nancy's desperation and her mounting feelings of anger. I felt "stuck" in our work but did not want to admit to my helplessness. Nancy's feelings of frustration grew until she, one day, hit her husband repeatedly when he woke her in the middle of the night.
> The abusive event made us both aware of the stalemate in treatment. I felt I had failed this client. I should have given more help, and given it sooner. I felt angry that she had

betrayed me, that she revealed my impotency as her helper. I told myself that Nancy was angry at me for reporting the abuse, and disappointed that I had let her down. I was ready for her to end our relationship. I was actually hoping she would terminate treatment so that I wouldn't have to face the aftermath, our anger and our failure. But Nancy did not leave treatment then. She still needed help. We still needed to talk about our helplessness and frustration, and to face the fact that, no matter how hard we tried, we couldn't fix her husband. As soon as we gave up the burden of finding a cure, I felt relieved and I think Nancy did too. Our work progressed slowly, but eventually Nancy was able to discover options for herself—a respite program and assistance from her adult children. She came to accept the fact that there was a limit to the amount of stress she could handle and that to get help for herself was a means of providing the best care for her husband. I, like Nancy, had to face one more time the fact that I had limits as a helper, and that I, too, could offer no more than my best effort.

Learning to Live with Loss

As helpers, we have the opportunity to assist our caregiving clients in recognizing their true feelings, yet in the process we can lose touch with our own. The primary implication for our work is that we must know our own feelings. We can do this by allowing ourselves some time after each meeting with our clients to experience what we have just been through, the painful world that we have been brought into. We can be alert to feelings of powerlessness, hopelessness, anger, and despair because these are indicators that something in us is stirring and that we may be feeling vulnerable.

Second, we can spend some time looking at similarities between our caregiver clients and ourselves or our past, current, or future life situations. The more similarities we find, the more likely we are to identify with our clients and the more likely we are to have our own values, beliefs, and feelings tested. If we are able to recognize these tests, these "hooks," in ourselves, we may be able to avoid detours and delays in our work or catch ourselves more quickly when we engage in struggles with our clients.

In essence, we need to learn to live with loss as a real life issue. Underneath so many of our clients' struggles are attempts to avoid the pain of loss, abandonment, and aloneness. As we come closer to uncovering the layers of powerlessness, denial, and despair within our clients, we come closer to seeing the loss in their lives, and in our own.

Early in my work with caregivers I had the privilege of working with Bob, a 56-year-old machinery technician. Bob was the youngest of three children; he grew up in a large, extended Italian-American family of migrant workers. He recalled his parents as being critical of him, and his father as being disappointed in him because he wasn't "macho," or "more of a man." Bob's first marriage at age 17 lasted for 12 years and he had four children. After his divorce from his first wife, he went through a period of heavy drinking and job instability. He saw his second marriage as a chance for him to get back on the right track and his new wife, Janet, as an "anchor." When I saw Bob, he had been married to Janet for 15 years, and reported that the marriage had been fraught with conflict for most of those years. Janet had contracted a debilitating illness that left her both physically and cognitively impaired. Bob cared for Janet for two years, alone on evenings and weekends and with home nursing help on weekdays.

Bob came for individual therapy because he felt depressed, angry, and abandoned by friends. He was also experiencing a number of stress-related physical complaints. But what became apparent after several meetings was Bob's fear of losing Janet. Bob was losing his anchor, and he wasn't sure of how he would survive without her.

Bob was in many ways an overinvolved caregiver struggling against his own powerlessness. He felt continually torn between his commitment to his job and to his wife, and was at serious risk of losing a job he enjoyed because he left work so often to see if his wife was still alive. The desperation he experienced anticipating her loss seemed beyond normal grief. He was experiencing separation anxiety and profound grief over losing his mainstay in life. As he watched her decline, he struggled with the fear that he would succumb to drinking, that without his anchor he could not care enough for himself to keep his life on the right track. The first task of our work was to have Bob realize that he needed to give himself permission to let go of his wife and permission to explore what his life would be like without his anchor. The therapeutic relationship became the arena for Bob to work through separating. Our work became a vehicle to learn about making a transition from a relationship and feeling a readiness to make that transition. Bob developed a sexualized transference to me. In this transference, Bob saw me as the most important woman in his life, as his new anchor. When Bob felt himself emotionally detaching from Janet, his fear emerged. He almost left treatment then, to return to investing all his energies into caring for her. Bob was repeating the pattern in his life of never fully letting go of relationships because he feared what the loss would mean to him. Through understanding this pattern, Bob finally decided to remain in treatment and confront, rather than act out, the fear of being alone.

My countertransference reactions to Bob varied during the course of our work. Initially, I felt positively toward him because of his devotion to his wife and his desire to do all he could for her. I identified with the helper in him. Eventually, though, I found myself feeling a pull to rescue him from his plight. My own need for connectedness surfaced as I realized that Bob's ambivalence about facing life alone was like my own. The task of letting go of a significant loved one was difficult both for Bob, who had not received enough nurturing early in life, and for me, because my father had died early in my childhood. Before the issues of loss and abandonment could be addressed, the sexualized transference developed and became the focus of several subsequent sessions. I felt distant from Bob and uncomfortable about his desire to over-step the boundaries of the therapy relationship. By under-standing Bob's transference as a reflection of his need for something to hold onto and a sign of his sense of aloneness, I worked through my initial negative feelings. Only then could I help both Bob and myself to see these sexual feelings as a manifestation of Bob's real need for physical and emotional closeness.

As I reflect back on my work with Bob, I recognize now that, although working with the sexual transference was important, it also served to distract both of us from the issue of loss. My countertransference reaction of wanting to avoid examining my losses contributed to delaying this important piece of therapeutic work. In time, Bob gradually came to recognize his own gift of being able to care for others and was able to feel comfortable with the more sensitive side of himself. He was able, by becoming his own anchor, to recognize and incorporate the accomplishments in his life, the times he did please his parents, the advances he made on his job, the people he had helped in his role as a technician supervisor, and all he had done for his wife as her caregiver and husband. By the end of therapy, Bob had been successful in reducing his level of overinvolvement but not his level of caring. He continued to provide excellent care for his wife with the help of home health aid services.

Terminating our work set the stage for talking about the loss of our work together and about how difficult it is to face the eventual but permanent loss of someone you love. At the end of the treatment, I remember saying goodbye to Bob and feeling proud of him. Bob had come to examine his fear of losing Janet, and to believe he was doing all he could for her. He was not sure how he would handle her death, but he had done preparatory work and seemed more able to handle his grief and survive it. I felt good at the end of treatment because of what I had learned from Bob: that people can face the loss of those they most love, and grow in the process.

Summary

Family caregivers and professional helpers encounter similar experiences when we work together. Identifying with caregivers can both help and hinder our work, depending on how we use the information our own feelings provide us. We may find that we mirror our client's experiences of powerlessness, hopelessness, anger, or denial that the loved one is ill. To confront loss in the lives of our caregiver clients, we must have the courage to face loss in our own lives. It is only when we uncover our own struggles, our own layers, and our own losses that we can truly face what is underneath these layers in our clients.

References

Gallagher, D., Rose, J., Rivera, P., Lovett, S., & Thompson, L. W. (in press). Prevalence of depression in family caregivers. *The Gerontologist*.

Gallagher, D., Wrabetz, A., Lovett, S., DelMaestro, S., & Rose, J. (1989). Depression and other negative affects in family caregivers. In E. Light & B. Lebowitz (Eds.), *Alzheimer's disease treatment and family stress: Directions for research*. Washington, DC: U.S. Government Printing Office.

Rose, J., & DelMaestro, S. (in press). Separation and individuation conflicts as a model for understanding caregiver distress. Psychodynamic and cognitive case studies. *The Gerontologist*.

10

Case Management:
Awareness of Feelings

IRENE WILLIAMS

Case managers assist older clients in getting the help they need in today's often complex and fragmented service system. Case management involves outreach, needs assessment, linking clients to services, and follow-up. Often, the goal of case management is keeping a frail older person at home and out of a nursing home as long as possible; but case managers also serve clients in institutions such as hospitals and nursing homes.

The case management function takes place in many different settings, each with different limits as defined by professional standards, legal regulations, agency policies, and by the personal ability and training of the individual worker. Case managers must keep up with a wide variety of technical information: available services, eligibility requirements, and paperwork needed for clients to qualify for services. As case managers we need to be in touch with the feelings we experience and their connections to the work we do and the services we deliver. Ann Burack-Weiss (1988) says:

> The theory of case management is technical. The practice of case management is emotional. The language of theory refers to systems, networks, supports, linkages, and tracking. The language of practitioners is of fear, anxiety, depression, and ambivalence. (pp. 23-25)

The personal reactions that hook us as we try to manage our feelings are major keys to helping clients (Katz & Genevay, 1987). Self-knowledge leads us to personal involvement and professional connection with the people we serve. The following three case studies illustrate how our personal feelings can both help and hinder effective case management, and how understanding these feelings can be vital to resolving difficult situations.

Eugenia:
Avoiding My Own Anger and Grief

My experiences with Eugenia illustrate several common countertransference issues that case managers face: wanting to avoid our own grief, wanting to avoid our own anger, fear of confronting more powerful staff members in the care system, and the growth for both client and case manager that can result from facing these feelings.

Eugenia was 84, diabetic, and blind. She came to a hospital, where I worked as a case manager, three times a week for dialysis. She lived in a skilled nursing home, and was tormented by illness and repeated invasive surgeries. She was scheduled soon to have an amputation. I found myself avoiding Eugenia's suffering and I even had a good excuse for doing so. One major reason for approaching clients was to assist with referrals for public benefits. Eugenia's dialysis and placement costs were already covered by MediCal; in fact, she had divorced her husband of 27 years to become eligible. My strong desire to avoid Eugenia was my clue to my own countertransference.

Working as a case manager in a hospital, I had already been forced to face some of my unresolved fears of death, helplessness, and loss of personal control. Each time I worked with a dying patient, I was aware of holding on to feelings left over from my experience with my mother's long illness and painful death, when I was just 14. This is not uncommon among caregivers (Genevay, 1987). With the help of good supervision, I was generally able to put aside personal feelings and to become really available to my clients in their last days. It was different with Eugenia.

Eugenia was the same age my mother would have been if she had lived. Seeing Eugenia, I again felt helpless and abandoned. There had been nothing I could do, back then, to ease my mother's suffering. I felt just as helpless with Eugenia. As I looked at Eugenia, I was reminded of the many times I had hesitated before entering my mother's hospital room. I felt scared of the choking smells and the small space which kept Mom (and now Eugenia) alive. I wanted to deny the presence of pain and loneliness, death's companions.

My first step forward was recognizing the ways that Eugenia was different from my mother. My mother died in 1943, and the technology surrounding her death was very different from that tormenting Eugenia. My mother had been "too young" to die—everyone said so. Eugenia was nearing the end of a long life. My mother had stayed married; Eugenia had divorced.

But I still had other complicated feelings to face before I could be of real help to Eugenia. Her suffering appalled me. She accepted any medical treatment, however painful, helplessly. Her stoicism made me feel helpless, too. Feeling useless as a professional, I judged her life as useless. I just wanted her to die and get it over with.

FINDING THE COURAGE

In order to deal with these feelings, I had to recognize how angry I was at the medical system that was prolonging Eugenia's life in such a painful way. I would have to work up the courage to confront her health care management team. I would have to talk to Eugenia about her options for refusing treatment, and she might not be receptive to me.

I spoke to the charge nurse first, then to other staff members. They said they were all feeling like me; they wanted to run away from Eugenia. Then I raised the questions in a staff planning session: Did she have to go through with all this surgery? And what would happen if she stopped dialysis? Her nephrologist said that without dialysis, she would die within two weeks. Everyone expressed conflict at that staff session, and her doctor needed to guard against possible charges of malpractice, but we finally agreed that Eugenia needed to know her options if she were to make a choice to stop treatment.

I was finally calm enough to approach Eugenia's bedside, but I still thought she might reject me, giving me a final excuse to go away. She was sleeping. Still feeling tentative about how I might react, I searched her face for any sign of response, recognition, or rejection. After all, she must have been aware that I had purposely avoided her. When she did not stir I started to move away, but she tightened her grasp of my hand and pulled me toward her. She wanted to say something. Slowly, she began to tell me about her only brother, who died with a similar disease. She was aware she would die in much the same way. Barely audible, she mourned both her brother and herself. My tears mixed with hers.

It turned out that Eugenia did not want her life prolonged by dialysis, and she did not want to spend her last days taking the drugs she would need to escape the pain of surgery. Her real pain was over something else. She was tormented by her divorce from George, her husband of 27 years. She wanted to die with integrity, but couldn't see how she could. She wanted to remarry George. Dying as a divorced woman felt like a disgrace to her family and a betrayal of her loving husband. She gave me her permission to contact her minister for his opinion about her conflict.

CLOSURE

I explained to Eugenia's minister that she had divorced George in order not to be a financial burden on her husband, but that she was near death and grieving for the loss of her marital relationship. The minister knew George, who was still living in the couple's cottage. The minister said he would be more than happy to solemnize the couple's relationship at Eugenia's nursing home. In the meantime, Eugenia talked to the doctor and signed a form to refuse the scheduled surgery. For Eugenia, the significance of her refusal meant that she would die with integrity and she would have enough time to re-unite with her family before saying goodbye.

Eugenia went from looking like a ghost to being a real personality, once she was able to talk about—and make—her choices. I was present on the day of Eugenia's second "wedding," and celebrated the occasion along with her family and most of the nursing home staff who were her inner circle during her final days. An aide wheeled Eugenia into the makeshift chapel, where her husband waited. George placed a garland of fresh flowers on her head and the couple repeated their vows. She died three days later.

My desire to avoid Eugenia completely turned around. In her last days, she became a wonderful teacher, showing me how to let go of her as a person in the present and to take another step in letting go of the past loss of my mother. Eugenia and I were both empowered by our relationship.

Gerry:
When Staff and Clients Mirror Family

Gerry's story shows how a case manager can constructively use similarities between her relationships with her family and those with her staff and clients.

Gerry's new job was largely undefined by the agency that hired her. She was to be a case manager for a residential complex with 100 occupants, most of whom were original tenants of the facility when it was new 15 years ago. The sense of community previously established by the director and board of directors flourished as the residents lived side by side over the years. However, residents were now older and feebler. The comfortable era was passing, and neither the administrator nor the board knew how to deal with the new problems presented by the residents and their immediate family caregivers.

When Gerry took the job, the director asked her to evaluate the long-term care needs of each resident. He needed Gerry to plan alternative living arrangements for long-time residents who were slipping from independence to faltering health. Gerry was asked to report back to her superior and to the facility's board regarding her progress. There were two objectives: to develop a program plan that would contain rising costs; and to provide improved, individualized services to the residents. A third objective was implied but not acknowledged: She was to save the director from the tough job of confronting some residents with the news that they would be moving.

HER BROTHER, HER BOSS

The facility's administrative system was a reflection of Gerry's own family of origin. She was an only daughter in a family of five boys. Here she was the only female and case manager in a facility with a male administrator and a male board of directors.

Soon, Gerry found herself enmeshed in conflicts that resembled those she had had with her family of origin. The director was critical of her assessments and the way she spent time with the residents. He didn't want to face the need for some of the clients to move, and hoped that creating Gerry's job could forestall that. Gerry had cared for her mother, who had Parkinson's disease, for years in her own home. Her brother had been critical of the way Gerry provided care. Later, Gerry became exhausted by caring for her mother and her children while also holding down a job. She placed her mother in a nursing home, and her brother objected to that, too, without being willing to take their mother into his home.

The director of the facility did not want to hire additional staff to care for increasingly frail residents, but he did not want to have to move anyone out, either. He hoped for a magic solution from Gerry. His vagueness about the goal of Gerry's work carried over from her reaction to her brothers' failure to provide for their mother's full-time care. When the director admonished her for wasting time with the residents, Gerry was doubly sensitive to her feelings of being criticized and dumped on. She had expected to experience some parent-child carryover in her work at the facility, but she was not prepared to deal with rivalry with siblings in her relationship with staff.

In the past, Gerry had often coped with stressful life situations by taking on too much responsibility. She described herself as a "Supermom" at home, with unlimited expectations of herself at work for high performance and achievement. For awhile she fell into the same trap, taking on too much in this ill-defined job. She felt guilty about her inability to solve all of the residents' problems regarding long-term care, and she became particularly anxious about the residents who would have to move.

But Gerry had learned to deal with criticism from her brothers, and now she was able to apply what she had learned to the impasse at her job. She gave up her perfectionistic standards and learned to give herself credit for the many ways in which she served the elderly residents and their families.

Instead of being deterred by the boss's criticism, she asked him to help her by taking on a role of "favorite son," and he became a regular visitor with Gerry whenever she had a difficult case. The collaboration that had not been possible with her own brothers was corrected by her ability to turn negative input into team energy.

She also devised ways for the facility's board to feel more included. She shared particularly difficult issues with them, and encouraged them to make policy decisions about either expanding services or moving residents out.

HER MOTHER, HER CLIENTS

There was another painful parallel for Gerry between her family and her job. As she became acquainted with the older clients and watched them fail, she could not help but feel sadness and grief at her mother's failing physical strength and dementia. She learned to deal with her mother's depleted memory by telling her mother about her own feelings of helplessness. She talked to her about her inner disappointments, even when her mother could no longer hear or respond to what she was saying. She found that as she shared her frustrations she was also able to express her appreciation and thanks for the wonderful human being now physically and mentally shriveling before her eyes.

Gerry's relationship with her mother allowed her to see ways she needed to drop her professional mask with her clients. She loosened up with the residents, and lessened her professional distance, finding important balance between warm caring and professional discipline.

Lorraine:
Pitfalls of Positive Countertransference

Case management is a mutual process of involvement and change. We engage in a similar process when we supervise students who are learning to be case managers. My experiences with Lorraine, a student intern I supervised, illustrate problems that positive countertransference feelings may present, whether they are directed toward colleagues or clients.

From my first meeting with Lorraine, a wide-eyed, 22-year-old, first-year graduate student, I liked her instantly. She had real enthusiasm for learning. Her interest in working with the elderly stemmed from very positive relationships with her own grandparents, and she had the cultural expectations that elders are to be regarded for their wisdom and prized for their experience. Because I was 60 years old, I warmed up to her flattering expectations that I would be a good mentor.

I was to learn, however, that my positive feelings toward Lorraine could interfere both with supervising her effectively and with Lorraine's and my ability to be helpful to clients.

Our first task was a home visit to assess the needs of Mr. and Mrs. Frank. As we pulled up to their small frame house, I was trying to deny my own anxiety. I had multiple tasks ahead of me: to demonstrate my working techniques to the student, to make an adequate assessment of our clients' needs, and finally to create a case plan that would meet my professional standards for training case managers. To quell my anxiety, I told myself this would be a pretty easy case, a gentle way to begin Lorraine's year of internship. From Lorraine's description of her phone intake with Mr. Frank, it seemed he needed help with his 84-year-old wife, a dementia patient who had recently taken to wandering. We would probably offer him respite care, a service our agency could provide.

As our interview with Mr. Frank began, everything did seem to go well. Both the Franks responded well to Lorraine's youthful interest. But because I wanted Lorraine to do well, I ignored her role as passive interested observer and took too much initiative myself. I also failed to notice that the talk with Mr. Frank was staying on a shallow, positive level. He was being charming, but he was talking too much and he was skirting something. He said he didn't know anything about Alzheimer's disease, a problem we could remedy with information. His real concerns emerged more slowly.

AVOIDING ELDER ABUSE

Mr. Frank explained that his wife had been a "bad girl" the past week. "She took off on me while I was fixing the doors to keep them locked. The bad thing about it was that when I found her three blocks away at a friend's house, she was flat out on the pavement. I was so scared, I just stood there in shock. Somebody else called the doctor."

He also told us that Mrs. Frank was having pains in her arms that made it more difficult for him to help her eat, dress, and bathe. I could sense some of his anger and frustration. The story of her fall and the anger he was expressing could be signs that he was covering up having contributed to his wife's injury. Mrs. Frank also seemed to be listening to the conversation for tones of disapproval, another possible sign that she was being abused. I was in the midst of showing Lorraine how to fill out our agency's 10-page assessment forms. Elder abuse would mean another set of forms, and I wasn't sure that the machinery of Adult Protective Services could be of any help in a case like the Franks'. I just didn't want to face the possibility of abuse. I didn't want to expose the Franks to that judgment if it wasn't necessary. I also wanted to protect Lorraine from facing a difficult situation.

My positive feelings for this couple could possibly have prevented them from getting the help they needed. My positive feelings for Lorraine could have prevented her experience of elder abuse reporting, a responsibility she was bound to face as a case manager. Lorraine, however, had a different set of feelings about elder abuse, and demonstrated her sensitivity as she spoke to Mrs. Frank.

Lorraine reached over to Mrs. Frank, asking to see her arms. Mrs. Frank revealed one especially bad bruise on her upper arm. Lorraine's concern was comforting to Mrs. Frank, and she smiled when Lorraine said: "It looks like you fell pretty hard there."

As we talked further with Mr. Frank, he described a visit by a social worker "who asked a lot of senseless questions." It occurred to me that the elder abuse report had already been made, which might account for the appearance of the other social worker. Mr. Frank became angry when he talked about the other social worker. I experienced a brief flare-up of a common, unspoken counter-transference reaction in difficult cases: rivalry with other professionals and their agencies. I had to admit I was caught—ever so slightly, but ever so decidedly—in the feeling that I was a better professional than the insensitive social worker who had intruded on the Franks. By blaming this other professional, I could preserve my positive feelings toward the Franks, and ward off the knowledge that my own student intern had one-upped me by confronting the possibility of elder abuse. I temporarily blocked out Mr. Frank's need for respite, and Lorraine's right to learn how to monitor her client's needs.

Mr. Frank became very defensive and said he didn't need any help with his wife's care. He spoke almost too much of his undying love for her; I felt the prior investigation of possible elder abuse had forced him to deny his real feelings of anger and helplessness. He insisted on showing us how safe he had made his wife's bedroom and bathroom. He reviewed with us the way he managed to keep his wife's medicines straight, and said he thought he could probably manage the continued care of his wife without an attendant worker coming in to help. After all, even if he knew that his wife was being properly cared for, he would have no place to go where he could relax. He seemed to be asking for personal reassurance more than for respite service. Based on an emergency need to prevent possible abuse, we left the interview with the understanding that Lorraine would arrange for immediate respite, and would follow up to reassess how the couple were using it.

AVOIDING GIVING CRITICISM

Contrary to my expectations, this first interview with Lorraine and the Franks had been very stressful and tiring for me. On the return drive back to the office, I felt disappointed when Lorraine did not praise my performance. I also found myself being less than honest with her, giving her unreasonable reassurances of doing a very good job. I showed appreciation for her skillful and tender intervention with Mrs. Frank, and I continued with more positive reinforcement regarding her recognition of elder abuse signals. I did not tell her that, with the exception of checking Mrs. Frank's injuries, she had been too passive, too much the observer. I also didn't explain to her honestly why I had preferred to avoid the question of elder abuse. I was feeling stressed, because I had taken most of the responsibility for the interview. Lorraine's response was to ask for tougher cases because she thought this one was too easy. I had protected her from the difficult parts.

We both continued to avoid my need to criticize some of her work. She was supposed to write a report on the case; she kept forgetting to bring it in. I let that go unchallenged. I was stuck, and the Franks were not getting help they might need. I talked the whole situation over with a trusted colleague, who made me realize I had to be honest and push Lorraine a little more. I insisted she bring in the report, and that she follow up on the case.

I asked Lorraine to call the social worker who had made the first visit to the Franks. Lorraine reported that the worker had been called in by the doctor, and had submitted a report showing no elder abuse. For the next two months, Mr. Frank received vouchered authorization for respite service. And during the same two months, he refused to accept it. The Franks still needed help, however, even if he refused respite services. I advised Lorraine to call regularly and just be available to this very lonely couple. Mr. Frank eventually got some help caring for his wife from a previously uncooperative daughter. I believe that Lorraine's continued show of interest and support led him to get this help, even if his pride prevented him from accepting help from an agency.

Lorraine learned a valuable lesson in case management: to stay with the client, to be present and available to learn what the client really needs. I also learned that I needed to be honest in evaluations of students, even those I like very much. Not monitoring their performance and not giving them needed criticism robs them of valuable learning experiences.

Summary

Our most uncomfortable feelings often point the way to personal growth and to better interventions as case managers. We frequently must deal with emotional reactions to our clients, and also with emotional reactions to other professionals in a complex care system. My experiences with Eugenia illustrate how a case manager overcoming grief, anger, and the fear of confronting other staff members can be of great value to a dying client. Gerry's story shows how a case manager can translate feelings from family relationships into more positive working relationships with staff and clients. My experiences with Lorraine illustrate how even positive feelings can sometimes get in the way of good case management and supervision.

References

Burack-Weiss, A. (1988). Clinical aspects of case management. *Generations, 12*(5), 23-25.

Katz, R. S., & Genevay, B. (1987). Older people, dying and countertransference. *Generations, 11*(3), 28-31.

Genevay, B. (1987). Loss of a mother, A personal account. *Generations, 11*(3), 39-41.

11

Being Old, Sexual, and Intimate: A Threat or a Gift?

BONNIE GENEVAY

Grandma stood in front of him, overmatching him pound for pound, and taller too, for she had a growth spurt . . . while he had shrunk . . . She glared up and spoke her piece into his face about how he was off at all hours tomcatting and chasing Lamartine again and making a damn old fool of himself.

"And you got no more whoopee to pitch anymore anyhow!" she yelled at last, surprising me so my jaw just dropped, for us kids all had pretended for so long that those rustling sounds we heard from their side of the room at night never happened. . . . I saw that tears were in her eyes. And that's when I saw how much grief and love she felt for him. And it gave me a real shock to the system. You see I thought love got easier over the years so it didn't hurt so bad when it hurt, or feel so good when it felt good. I thought it smoothed out

and old people hardly noticed it. I thought it curled up and died, I guess. Now I saw it rear up like a whip and lash.
    She loved him. She was jealous. She mourned him like the dead. . . . She'd always love him . . . That hit me like a ton of bricks . . . I never loved like that . . . I wanted to go out and find a woman who I would love until one of us died or went crazy. (Erdrich, 1984, pp. 192-193)

Introduction

Great courage is required as we age to search out intimate relationships that are meaningful and to repair old intimacies that have gone astray. Intimacy needs are lifelong, and require a tapestry of significant relationships that confirm our identity and help us know who we are. (Genevay, 1986, p. 15.)

In our roles as helping professionals we manifest a great variety of responses toward old people who act sexual or let us know they have intimacy needs. Some of us—with fear and trembling—are willing to explore sensual-sexual-intimacy deficits with older clients and patients. Others of us would rather translate the sexual needs of elderly as socialization needs because it's more comfortable for us and we have more answers. We would rather prescribe for biological symptoms than emotional distress. For example, it may be easier to say "let me prescribe something for the dryness of your vagina" instead of "how long has it been since you've loved someone . . . can you tell me your worries about that now?" This last approach would lead us into emotional areas of sexuality we may feel least competent in.

Some of us hope sex won't rear its ugly head in "our" patients! This may be due to lack of training or knowledge, or to the fact that we may never have been very comfortable with our own sexuality, or because we are depressed about, or temporarily arrested in, our own sexual growth due to divorce, widowhood, or lack of a loving partner. We may have such a deep void in our own experience of being intimate with others that it is intimidating to work with older people who have a similar deep void in their lives. Or at times we may feel the awe of children at their parents' sexuality when older men and women let us view a glimpse of their very rich and deep patterns of sexual and intimate expression and experience.

This chapter will use a very broad brush to address a continuum of behaviors, beginning with sensory and sensual expression, through thoughts and feelings, sexual activity, and closeness with others—mental, emotional, physical and spiritual. Here are two examples which have ramifications far deeper than genital sexual expression.

THE THREAT

Victor had lost his wife recently, seemed depressed and docile, and had proved to be a pleasant client for the home health worker, Tina. One day Victor greeted Tina at the door with only his shirt on. She tried to ignore this, thinking he was in the midst of dressing. After she entered his home she became aware of lewd pictures Victor had placed around the living room. He then propositioned Tina, and insisted she have sex with him. Tina left the house very quickly, went directly to her supervisor, and asked that the case be transferred to someone else.

Tina was especially vulnerable at that time because her marriage was deteriorating, and she couldn't tolerate another demanding male in her life. Fortunately, for both Tina and Victor, the supervisor declined to transfer the case and went with Tina to Victor's home. She explained that if Tina left abruptly and failed to discover the reasons for his behavior it would increase Victor's depression and grief. She said that Tina needed experience in confronting the inappropriate behavior and handling it in a professional manner. Victor was fully clothed when they arrived, and in a state of extreme shame and guilt. He was in a crisis much more comprehensive than sexual acting-out, and Tina was able to refer him to mental, emotional, and grief services. She told him, eventually, that she liked him very much as a person but felt assaulted by his behavior, and Victor was able to apologize to her, saying he was "not himself" at the time. This case describes the threat—even the violation—older clients' inappropriate sexual expression can pose for us when their stress is extreme and their behaviors get out of control.

THE GIFT

Jan was a human services worker who had experienced a lot of pain in relationships with men throughout her life. But she had one particularly positive inheritance in the arena of intimacy. As a girl of eight she had come home from school early one day when no one expected her. Her grandparents lived with the family, and shared a small room with two twin beds in it. Jan's grandmother, who was frail and often ill, was usually passive, tired, and noncommunicative. On this occasion no voices greeted Jan's arrival home and she went to search for her grandparents, who rarely left the house. Running into their room, she found both of them in one twin bed looking flushed, shocked, and surprised. Her grandfather said, "We're just taking a little nap, honey. Wait outside and we'll be out in a minute." Jan says she will never forget the look of happiness on her grandmother's rosy face, nor the light and twinkle in her eyes. This was a family member she didn't often remember as being happy, and it impacted Jan deeply to see her grandmother in a state of pleasure, smiling and full of energy for the moment.

As an older woman herself, many years later, Jan said she had never lost that image of her grandparents as vital, alive people still loving each other. "Neutered, annihilated people can only live vicariously" (Melamed, 1983, p. 126). Jan's grandparents were not living vicariously. They were still on occasion tasting the fruits of their long partnership in ways adapted to their illness, disability, and aging. This, then, is the potential gift that older people—clients, our friends, our own older family members—can give to us when they model the expression of love and affection.

Professional helpers frequently reject this gift for a variety of reasons, including the fact that some old people themselves internalize the message that it's bad to express love if they're old—so they forego sexual and affectional interaction. "Do I hear whispers, 'Disgusting, those old people making love?' . . . we are merely ourselves, speaking, feeling, touching, loving in our differences as human beings" (Mannes, 1968, p. 58).

Ageist and Countertransferential Rationales

There are cultural and emotional reasons for this reluctance and blindness toward old people and intimacy on the part of professional helpers. Our underlying biases rest on societal and personal-professional foundations:

(1) We are participants in an ageist North American culture which devalues older people. Among the strongest mandates of youth-and-beauty worship is our denigration of people who are wrinkled, fat, bald, skinny, gray, old-looking, or disabled when they act like sexual beings;

(2) Many of us are uncomfortable with our own sexual and intimacy needs and feelings, and are greatly affected by the developmental stages of life we find ourselves in. For example, if you are 50 and divorced, with no present intimacy in your life, you may indeed have trouble listening to an 85-year-old talk about sexual expression in a marriage of 60 years. If you have recently been widowed at a young age, you may not want to deal with your parents' sexual closeness or with the loneliness and depression of a client who has just lost a partner at age 70. If you have never found sexual intimacy vital to your well-being—at any age—you may not want to listen to an elderly man or woman talk about vaginal discomfort, prolapse, premature ejaculation, prostatectomy, incontinence, or fears about erection. And you may have difficulty understanding the fact that those sexual-affectional behaviors which are habitual for older people contribute to their mental, emotional, and physical health. In addition, many of us have ill, disabled, and elderly parents, grandparents, and friends who run the gamut from being sexually active to intimacy-deprived, and we simply don't know how to cope with this personally. It is hard for most of us to even imagine our parents as sexual beings.

NEGATIVE STEREOTYPES OF OLDER WOMEN

Because there is a double standard of aging, spelled out long ago by Susan Sontag (1972), women are still penalized sexually at a younger age than men. Men are considered sexually eligible even after they become gray or wrinkled, while women are "past their prime" in many aspects of our culture as soon as that first wrinkle appears. So special consideration needs to be paid by practitioners to women who become asexual and invisible when they are old— or look "old."

In all my years of working with older women I have experienced most of them being more and more choosy and selective of partners as they age—not less selective. Regardless of the fact that our societal myth says they are lucky to receive any sexual attention at all in old age, their experience in loving and living with partners often makes them highly discriminating and unwilling to settle for second best. Older women who are our patients and clients have deep intimacy needs that professional helpers do not address, and often legitimately cannot fill. I speak here to both male and female practitioners, for we are socialized in the same ageist/sexist ways and have our own personal same-sex and opposite-sex blind spots and biases. The repulsion, sadness, fear, and empathy, which you and I often feel at hearing fantasies and confessions from older women, are frequently handled badly by many of us. This is due partly to the fact that (1) we are taught little or nothing about sexuality and intimacy as it relates to older people, and (2) we are intimidated when we are asked to respond to the lifelong intimacy needs of people who are the ages of our parents and grandparents. We get little encouragement to look at our countertransference reactions from supervisors, administrators, and colleagues.

SEXUAL AND AFFECTIONAL CHOICE WITHOUT PROFESSIONAL PUNISHMENT

In a large nursing home one resident became uptight about another woman who very frequently touched and held hands, as well as hugged, other female residents. The hugger was a warm, tender, and uninhibited person who appeared to accept her body deterioration with equanimity. The uptight woman accused the hugger of being lesbian, and was successful in her smear campaign against the affectionate woman, who became socially ostracized in the home. This happens . . . but only with support from whomever has the power—in the agency, institution, hospital or office—to collude with vicious and dehumanizing sexual myths and fears (Solnick, 1978). There is no way of knowing what the beliefs and fantasies of the staff were in connection with this affectionate older resident. Nor what cultural and family rules and stereotypes of their own dictated the staff's allowing gossip and isolation to grow from one resident making assumptions about another.

One lesbian professional pointed out how words distort human experience.

In a national news special on homosexuality, the term "practicing homosexuals" was used. This smacks of the disease model—something to be "cured of," for we don't speak of "practicing heterosexuals." We *expect* heterosexuals to practice sexual expression. If we expect older gay clients and patients to transcend their fears and current cultural prejudices, we need to sift through our words, nuances of gesture, facial expression, and bodily avoidance (Solnick, 1978).

An older gay man was dying of congestive heart failure in the intensive care unit of a hospital. A staff member observed another older man hold his hand and give him a hug. Soon after the visitor was told that only family members related by blood or marriage were allowed in intensive care, and that he would have to leave. He begged to stay, saying he was a very close long-time friend of the patient, but the staff person was adamant that unless he were a parent, brother, sister, or spouse, he had to leave. The patient died alone. His visitor was his partner of over 20 years—but did not qualify as "spouse" in the perception of this particular helping professional.

As helpers we need to look at our personal and familial sexual stereotypes and how they potentially hinder our communication. We need to look at the ways in which we approach older men and women that disallow their unique sexual identities. In what ways do we offend? How do we cut off any possible communication to us about the life history of the person we are seeking to serve? How do our fears of people different from ourselves impede our diagnosis and treatment? How does our homophobia or limited life experience with people of sexual orientations other than our own affect the work we do?

Personal-Professional Connections

Listen to the personal-professional connections, the counter-transference issues, that surround our own timeless and ageless thoughts, feelings, and behaviors about intimacy and sexuality. They include sexual expression and repression, identity, self-esteem, touch deprivation, and inclusion/exclusion. We will elaborate on sexual expression and repression, and touch deprivation. Our discussion pays homage to the concept of "the second language of sex," which is emotional and communicative as well as physical (Butler & Lewis, 1978, p. 180).

SEXUAL EXPRESSION AND REPRESSION:
HANK AND MAUDE.

Hank, 87, was a widower for many years. He had remained celibate after his wife's death until after his prostatectomy, when he discovered to his great joy that he could still achieve an erection. He shared with Peggy, his outreach worker, that he felt like loving someone again for the first time in a long time. In her forties and divorced, Peggy encouraged Hank to find another partner. He said he felt his middle-aged daughter would think he was unfaithful to their mother. And he was afraid to consider his next-door neighbor, a woman he had been fond of for years, because others would disapprove. But he did say that he had fantasies about sleeping with his neighbor "now and again." Some time later, following the verbal intimacy between Peggy and Hank, which had evolved from sharing his desires, Hank asked Peggy if she would like him to make *her* happy. "I know how hard it must be for you to be alone," he said, "and I am really a fine lover. My wife always told me so. I know many different ways of loving."

Peggy found herself speechless. As an open, nonjudgmental person she had no problems with Hank's need for intimacy or with his high sexual self-esteem. But she had encouraged him to find a partner so he would choose someone "his own age," not herself. Taken aback, all she could think of to say was, "Thank you, Hank, for thinking of me, but it's just not possible at this time." You may think at this juncture that Peggy should never have listened to Hank or encouraged him to find a partner. But this was an integral part of her philosophy of helping older people with intimacy deficits.

Concerned only that she might have acted inappropriately with Hank in some way, she thought through their relationship and then visited him several days later. Checking this out with Hank, she discovered that he did not feel she had led him on in any way. He said he simply was a courageous fellow, and had decided he would never forgive himself if he didn't at least try. He said he'd never had a "worker" before, so he didn't know the protocol when he wanted to express his affection. Peggy told him that she found him intelligent and charming, and hoped that what had happened would in no way affect her work with him. He said, "No, . . . but you don't know what you're missing!" He winked at her and requested a service he thought her agency could provide. Convinced that she acted professionally in addressing this situation, being sure she had not hurt his feelings, and making certain his self-worth was intact, Peggy felt competent and professional. Their relationship was a close and honest one for the remainder of Hank's life.

In consultation with a colleague on this case, Peggy acknowledged that ageism was part of her feeling toward Hank's offer. Even if he had not been "the client" and she "the helper," and even if she had not been concerned about contaminating a warm, professional relationship with Hank, she found she could not imagine herself loving anyone 40 years older than herself. This produced an interesting ethical discussion about ageism, classism, and feelings of intellectual superiority toward older clients in Peggy's staff case consultation group. It centered around older-younger relationships, and the kind of judgments about men and women in nontraditional relationships that affect practice.

As a verbally expressive man Hank had the ego strength and self-confidence to pursue a relationship, and the emotional stability to cope with rejection despite the many losses in his life. Contrast him with Maude, a woman in her early seventies, who had a history of child abuse, sexual and emotional abuse by one husband, and a long caregiving experience with another husband during which she received no affection, touching, or closeness of any kind for years.

Maude attended a workshop on sexuality for older women, and sat silently throughout the morning as the leaders spoke about "using it or losing it," the importance of massage, masturbation, and the need for older women to be assertive in finding partners by extending invitations to men first, rather than waiting to be asked. Finally Maude raised her hand and said, "You've been talking about all these sexually explicit things. I can't even get up the courage to ask a *man or a woman* to meet me for a cup of coffee! I'm so afraid they'll reject me that I just sit and wait to be noticed. How can I ever get to the point of thinking about dating or companionship when I'm too afraid to say hello?"

The leaders of this workshop had not known the wide range of loneliness and deprivation felt by some participants in the workshop until Maude had the courage to speak. Her powerful statement enabled the leaders to backtrack and address the sexual repression of older people whose personal losses, family history, family rules about intimacy, and low self-esteem make it impossible for them to act on their closeness needs.

The personal-professional connection means not only enabling people like Maude to inform us about their uniquely repressed experiences with intimacy, but also becoming aware that if we come from families where there has been no evidence of affection, or healthy sexual expression, it is hard for us to give permission to old people to pursue intimacy. I frequently ask the professionals I train what messages they received from their parents, grandparents, and other family members about intimacy. Common responses go something like this: "I have no idea if my parents had much sex." "There wasn't much closeness in our family." "I hardly ever saw my parents hug, and I've never even been sure if they loved each other." Is it any wonder that those of us who come from dysfunctional families of many kinds have difficulty working with trust and intimacy issues with older people? We have often had no permission ourselves to be fully human males and females in our own lives, and continue to struggle with this ourselves. How much we need older people who are comfortable with their sexuality to be examples and to teach us about options and possibilities.

Here is an exercise I have used in training that you may wish to experiment with yourself, or use with your staff.

1. Breathe deeply, close your eyes, and spend a few minutes reflecting on the messages *you* received about sex and intimacy from your family.
2. Now try to be in touch with those attitudes and biases which hinder your openness to differences you may encounter in the older people you work with.
3. Shift your focus and imagine what messages you would *like* to give yourself and others, including older clients and patients.
4. Visualize the kind of growth and training that would be useful to you in the area of intimacy and sexuality.

This kind of reflection is one way to begin addressing counter-transference issues. It may lead you to provide staff training on intimacy and aging, to read further on the subject, to discuss them with colleagues, to consult with others, to initiate a professional staff support group, or possibly to obtain therapy for yourself.

TOUCH DEPRIVATION AND AUTHENTICITY

One of the most difficult things for us as practitioners is to be true to our own natural and authentic inclinations about touching others, hugging or not hugging and being physically close or physically distant. Most of us have mastered the socially correct "polite" handshake, but there are some whose clammy hands and fishy handshakes reveal that they really would prefer not to shake hands. For these people I think it is more honest to project warmth in some other way—through the *voice* or the *eyes*, rather than *touching* people in a way that gives a double message. Again this has to do with such past life experiences as habits in the family, cultural injunctions, previous personal experience of violation, and learned behavior.

When clients and patients are experiencing touch deprivation, we must be responsible and therapeutic by engaging in the most honest communication possible. This means *not* hugging someone if we don't feel like it. Not touching is valid behavior with an affection-starved older person who may read far too much into affectional behaviors on our part, or misunderstand our intentions. Our words frequently lie, but it is harder to lie with the body. To engage in hand-touching, back-patting, or hugging around the shoulders that is not meaningful to both client and helper is a disservice; it is neither respectful to the client nor to ourselves. Some of us are touchers, and some of us are not. For people who are very comfortable with holding, hugging, touching, and kissing, and who clearly check out their clients' personal and spatial boundaries so that they do not violate their clients, human touch is one of the most healing and healthful of communication exchanges.

There need be no preferred way to provide closeness and caring toward touch-deprived people. The challenge is to be in touch with the needs of clients, to check out with them what is and is not helpful, to respond as honestly as we can, and not to promise intimacy we cannot fulfill, whether it is expressed with words, or gestures, or body language.

I will never forget the client who opened her front door for me and then stood in the doorway, while inviting me in, so I had to press past her to get into the house. It took many visits before I learned that her husband had walked out on her many years hence, and that her dog had died some time before. She described herself as a woman who always loved to hug people, and then said, "But I'll be damned if I'll hug first! If they don't want to be close to me—forget it." She was unaware of her deep need for closeness and how she manipulated the situation to get physical closeness. Since I am not put off by contact with the human body, I did not feel violated by her forcing me to touch her shoulder, arm, and hip. But if I *had* felt violated and not addressed it, it is possible that she would have felt my repugnance and I would never have gotten to know her loneliness and feelings of rejection and defiance. She did not consciously wish to violate my personal space, and this encounter brought forth some interesting work by the two of us. We struggled with options for her to be in closer touch with others. This resulted in a deeper level of honesty about other issues. I would have missed a great opportunity for counseling if we had not talked about the way she let me in her house, and I might have terminated her prematurely because of my negative countertransference reaction to her hunger for touching.

Personal-Professional Dilemmas

FEELING ATTRACTED TO A CLIENT

Emma was a very skilled geriatric therapist. She'd had early experience with sex in her own life and was quite comfortable with both men and women. She found herself attracted to many of the older men who were her clients, and justified this by saying, "I just love all old people!" The first time she allowed herself to know it was sexual attraction she felt, Emma told a colleague, "I can't believe it . . . he has brown spots all over his skin, he has rough and calloused hands, puffy eyes, and he's on his sixth pacemaker! How *could I possibly* be attracted to him?" Her colleague said, "That's pretty surface stuff. What else do you like about him?" Emma then began to describe the fascinating life he'd lived, the obstacles he'd overcome, his courtesy, and his sensitivity to her as a person. Emma's friend replied, "He sounds like quite a man! Guess you were just born in the wrong generation."

The friend's easy acceptance of this sexual attraction to a man many years older enabled Emma to see that sexual energy is timeless and ageless. It challenged her skin-deep definition of sexual attraction, and helped her to feel okay about her feelings. "As long as you don't *act* on it, there's nothing wrong with caring about a sexy man who's your client," the friend said. "Do you want to go to bed with him?" At first glance this seemed like a crude question to Emma, but it turned out not to be so. After thinking about it Emma replied, "No! I just want to treat him like the fine person he is, and share a little of my warmth and energy with him. Maybe it will help him tolerate this last pacemaker." You may wish to stop here for a moment and recall what you *felt*, *thought*, and *did* the last time you were attracted to a client or patient.

WHEN A CLIENT ASKS TOO MUCH

Phillip was a young geriatric in-home health worker who called himself a "loner." He was seeing an older woman, obese and disabled, for monitoring of blood pressure, and symptoms of diabetes and depression. Mary, his patient, was fond of Phillip and looked forward to his visits. Suddenly on one visit, Mary said, "I want you." Phillip ignored this, but on his following visit Mary repeated it several times. Phillip joked with her, then terminated the visit early, and sought consultation from his supervisor.

Phillip and the supervisor discussed that he could say no to Mary, or leave at any point when his personal boundaries were being violated, but that he would have to be clear and honest with Mary and treat her in a respectful way. She suggested that Phillip didn't really know *what* it was Mary wanted, and urged him to go back and clarify it. Did Mary want a surrogate son? Did she want Phillip to spend more time with her as a friend? Did she want a sexual liaison?

When Phillip initiated the conversation, and asked Mary exactly what she wanted, she couldn't verbalize it. Suddenly she burst into tears and told Phillip she wanted someone to hold her. He felt awkward about this, but put his arm around her shoulders as he sat next to her. The physical closeness allowed Mary to experience her loneliness and isolation. "I'm all alone," she said, "and it's been so long since anyone held me. I miss my father . . . he used to hold me and cuddle me when I was a little girl." Phillip became uncomfortable for a minute or two, not wishing to be Mary's "father," but during that time realized that Mary probably didn't want anything of him that he couldn't give. Sensitive to Phillip's silence, and feeling guilty that she might be taking too much of his time, Mary said, "Thank you. I'll be all right now." Relieved that he could respond to her, Phillip tightened his hug and gave her a warm smile. This was a nonverbal way of concluding intimacy and saying goodbye for this time, and Phillip's self-confidence in handling sticky situations grew.

This was also an appropriate patient-helper communication, which paved the way for Mary to engage in more life review. So often life review is anchored by intimate events throughout the lifespan, and occurs when a helper is willing to risk and to use her- or himself as a "vehicle" for furthering the client's understanding. Phillip admitted later that he was very intimidated when Mary said "I want you." But his supervisor's consultation and support made it possible for him to pursue the meaning of the situation. It was a breakthrough for Phillip because he trusted himself more to work through his own limits, and to be very clear with himself. He knew that in the future he could say, "Yes, I can hold and rock you for a little while," or "No, I wish I could help, but that wouldn't be comfortable for me." Phillip referred Mary for in-home counseling because of his own limited life experience with intimacy, but he remained an affectionate support for her in his role of geriatric health worker.

WHEN WE HAVE AFFECTIONAL VOIDS OF OUR OWN

Rose was at a point in her life when she was starved for affection. Her husband had been abusive, and when she had divorced him many years before she'd poured all her love into her relationship with her two children. Now grown, the children lived at a distance and were not as attentive as she'd like. Rose felt personally as if she'd aged prematurely: Her hair was graying, her figure was becoming matronly, and it had been a long time since she had been out with a man socially. Joe was one of her favorite patients in the adult day center where she worked, and he lavished verbal attention on Rose. When Joe began to sit close to, and occasionally fondle, another participant in the program Rose became angry. She complained to many of the staff that Joe was exploiting a participant who could not defend herself. The only evidence to the contrary was that the woman smiled a lot whenever Joe was around her, and seemed to seek him out whenever she could. Rose called Joe "a dirty old man" and refused to do anything for him.

A social worker with the program checked out the understanding and feelings of the other participants in the program and Joe's family. None of the other people in the program seemed upset—certainly not as violated as Rose seemed—and some of them enjoyed the couple vicariously. Joe's family said they could understand Joe's actions, because he had missed the companionship of their mother since she'd died. The administrator of the program tried to help Rose understand what was going on, and asked her to avoid any further maligning of Joe. Rose began to see that her own affectional void, and the possibility that she might be jealous—because Joe had paid a lot of attention to Rose previously—could have contributed to her perceptions and behaviors. The administrator encouraged Rose, a fine worker, to utilize her employee assistance benefits and to get counseling for herself. An inservice training on intimacy, for the entire staff of the day center, focused on the issue that when helpers are bereft of intimacy in their own lives, it is natural for them to have a hard time observing a wealth of intimacy in other people—old or young. The trainer concluded with, "the key is in letting ourselves know that we are indeed affected greatly by the behaviors of others—staff, clients, friends and family. Searching out the countertransference reactions, and looking at where we are in our own lives, is a healthy and professional response."

HANDLING SCARY SITUATIONS

Max was a minister who spent part of his time as chaplain in a nursing home. One of his favorite patients was a dignified man who wore a feather in his hat. This man, Lester, was in a state of confusion but had retained just enough conversational cliches from his past memory to carry on limited, repetitive dialogue. One day, as Max sat beside Lester near the nurses' station, Lester unfastened his trousers and began masturbating vigorously. For a moment Max was shocked and mesmerized; then his values about public display of sexual expression surfaced and he fastened his eyes on Lester's so he wouldn't have to watch this unseemly behavior. He longed to flee down the hall, but was glued to the spot because he didn't know what he should do and felt extremely out of control. Max wasn't used to terminating a visit without shaking hands, yet there was no way he felt he could shake hands with Lester at that point. And Max also felt Lester's vulnerability; he didn't want to leave Lester alone to possible judgment by others.

As he glanced around Max saw no one observing, but he kept hoping a nurse or an aide would come and rescue him. Max somehow felt as guilty as if *he* had been caught masturbating. Then it occurred to him that he had been severely punished in his growing up years for this very activity, and that he was still angry about the treatment he'd received.

Eventually a warm and kind staff member walked by and nonintrusively put a large towel over Lester's lap, as he smiled at Max and said, "I'll get his wheelchair and take him into his room so you can have a longer visit." "No," Max said, "I've had enough for today," and he meant that on many different levels.

An insightful man, Max reflected on his reactions to Lester, and mentally played out the options open to him if this happened to him again. He decided it was time, in middle age, to let go of his punitive feelings about masturbation. He differentiated between believing that masturbation was a normal activity, and not wanting to witness what was a private and personal experience. He realized that Lester had no one in the world to love or touch him, and that self-touch might provide a great deal of comfort to a man who was confused and alone. At the next nursing home staff meeting Max inquired about what kind of consultation and inservice training was available to all levels of staff which would protect the privacy of residents and the dignity of confused people.

Checking Out Our Own Perceptions

We have many misperceptions about intimacy and older people. Some are due to our fear of not having all the answers to all the questions. How could we possibly have all the answers in an area as deep and awesome as intimacy? It is only our unrealistic professional perfectionism that misguides us into believing that if we were "good helpers" *we would know everything*. How could I, when I was 32, know what my mother grieved for most when she was widowed at 68? There is no law against learning from our clients and patients—and that is exactly what we have to do when we are 20, 30, or 50 and our clients are 80 and 100. Older people can teach us a great deal about love and intimacy *if* we wish to listen, and if we ask questions instead of giving "answers" that miss the mark because they are based on assumptions. Consider approaches like these:

"Tell me how it is for you? I really want to know."

"How long have you been alone?"

"What do you miss most?"

"Tell me what that means to you. I want to understand better, and I haven't had as much experience with this as you have . . ."

"Can I tell you what I think you mean? And then you can correct me if I'm wrong."

Failure to check out our perceptions leads to all kinds of assessment, referral, treatment, and service provision that is tangential and inappropriate. For example, a man was referred to a senior center for socialization when he was so blocked with grief over the loss of 40 years of an intimate marriage that there was no possibility he could socialize until he had done grief work.

Put yourself in the following situation. May is a disabled woman in her 70s.

MAY:	I want to talk to you about this man who rents a room in my daughter's house. (Pause)
COUNSELOR:	(Pause) Yes, . . . uh . . . exactly what happened?
MAY:	Nothing—yet. It's just that he seems to . . . well . . . he's a widower and has been alone a long time. When I go to stay with my daughter he. . . .
COUNSELOR:	(interrupting) Let's see, your daughter lives in Encino, doesn't she? That must be quite a trip for you.
MAY:	Yes, it is. It's painful to travel sometimes, and I wonder about living so far away from her.
COUNSELOR:	I've been meaning to talk to you about your present housing, May. It's important that you anticipate a more protected living environment, in preparation for the time when you . . . (Kirkpatrick, 1982, p. 98)

Needless to say, May did not bring up the incident with the widower again. Clearly her feelings about this man were not to be part of this counseling situation. If I were May, I'd wonder if my counselor were saying, "Cool it! Forget about men and prepare for total disability!" (Kirkpatrick, 1982, p. 98)

Put yourself now into the shoes of the counselor. Ask yourself:

1. What is *my* fantasy about what May wanted to say?
2. What are my feelings about wanting to hear that?
3. Would I have interrupted May's disclosure, because of my own discomfort, as this counselor did?
4. What are my attitudes about disabled older people expressing themselves sexually? Being exploited by others?
5. What might May have said that would be hard for me to listen to?

Here is another exercise which you might find helpful in relation to countertransference and intimacy:

You and I are aging. Each of us has unique experiences of closeness and intimacy in our own lives. Most of us have received some good—and perhaps some negative and very strange—messages from our family members and our culture about sexuality and intimacy. Some patients and clients remind us of good and of poor role models in our own families; others remind us of ourselves. The following questions are meant to stimulate your personal-professional connections.

Relax and reflect on your answers to the following questions:

1. In what ways do you accept your own psyche and body so that you can be at peace with your intimacy needs and expression?
2. In what ways do you affirm older people and give them permission to broaden their sexual and intimacy options?
3. How easy—or how difficult—is it for you to touch older people? In what ways do you touch them, and what is the meaning to you?
4. What fears do you have about talking to old people about sex and intimacy?
5. What fears do you have of talking to people of a sexual preference different from your own? In what ways do you attempt to see the person underneath the sexual preference?
6. How do you respond in terms of intimacy to people who are ugly (whatever that means to you), asexual, aggressively sexual, disabled, ill, dying? To people of a different religion or ethnic origin than your own?
7. In what ways do you affirm or deny your parents' sexuality? What messages from your family—verbal or nonverbal—are you still carrying around that are no longer useful to you? (adapted from Solnick, 1978, pp. 23-24)

Summary

If we are sexual beings to the end of our lives, then where are we to take this very precious and uniquely personal gift? Who will be the receivers of our affection, companionship, our touching and baring of innermost selves, our sharing of those parts which happen to be genital, our remembrance of our own sexual history? Who will hear us, touch us, and be pleased that we touch them—with words or hands or eyes—when we are old? (Solnick, 1978, p. 14)

If you let yourself be aware of, acknowledge, and consult your personal-professional connections to the intimate behaviors, thoughts, and feelings of old people, you will enhance your professional skills. But much more than that, you are creating a self-fulfilling prophecy for your own old age. Whether the intimacy of old people—observed, talked about, or personally encountered—is a *threat* to you as a helping professional, or a *gift* to you as you grow old is up to you. At the heart of countertransference is your ability to understand and respond to the feelings and closeness needs of older participants and clients, and that only happens when you learn from the people you serve and make connections between yourself, your parents and family, and your clients and their families. Being old means being sexual and intimate—in whatever ways have always defined our core identity, and to the degree we are able to manage in the midst of multiple losses.

Perhaps only in later life, when personality reaches its final stages of development, can love-making and sex achieve the fullest possible growth. Sex does not merely exist after sixty; it holds the possibility of becoming greater than it ever was. It can be joyful and creative, healthy and health-giving. (Butler & Lewis, 1976, p. 248.)

References

Butler, R., & Lewis, M. (1977). *Sex after sixty*. Boston: G. K. Hall.
Butler, R., & Lewis, M. (1978). The second language of sex. In R. L. Solnick (Ed.), *Sexuality and aging* (pp. 176-183). Los Angeles: University of Southern California Press.

Erdrich, L. (1984). *Love medicine*. New York: Holt, Rinehart & Winston.

Genevay, B. (1986). Intimacy as we age. *Generations, 10*(4), 15.

Kirkpatrick, M. (Ed.). (1982). In praise of older women. *Women's sexual experience-explorations of the dark continent* (p. 98). New York: Plenum Press.

Mannes, M. (1968). *They*. New York: Doubleday.

Melamed, E. (1983). *Mirror, mirror—The terror of not being young*. New York: Linden Press/Simon and Schuster.

Solnick, R. (Ed.). (1978). *Sexuality and aging*. Los Angeles: University of Southern California Press.

Sontag, S. (1972, September 23). The double standard of aging. *Saturday Review, The Society*.

12

The Older Worker and Ageism: Personal and Professional Dynamics

LOUISE BERNSTEIN

Ageism, or negative feelings about old age and the elderly, is a major problem continually dealt with in the field of gerontology. To look at countertransference in the older practitioner, I will first consider how ageism can impact the older worker's self-regard and ability to recognize and deal with ageism when it affects clients. Then, I will examine ways in which we can make use of the older worker's sensitivity and awareness.

Ageism and the Older Practitioner

There is no single definition of old age. I often begin talks to seniors by telling them about my experience of being asked by the local librarian whether I was entitled to a discount because of my age. She did not know what the "magic number" was. The Older Americans Act uses 55 for some programs, 60 for others, while our local senior cards are issued at 62 and Medicare begins at 65. Everyone knows people in their seventies and eighties who cannot really be considered old. So the decision about who is old is at best inconsistent, and there is still a widely held assumption that, whatever "old" may be, practitioners are not there yet. Carol Meyer (1986) tells us: "This is one stage of life that we can be assured no working professional has lived through; thus, it requires learning and often some stretching to achieve the empathy needed to be able to work comfortably and effectively with the aged." I find this puzzling and misleading. I can scarcely believe that Meyer does not know that some of us are already old and know firsthand how it feels! Bob Knight (1986), in his book *Psychotherapy with Older Adults*, discusses countertransference, problems that might arise with young and middle-aged therapists but does not at any point consider problems of elderly therapists. In his case illustrations, he assumes that the therapist who deals with older clients will be younger. In *Vital Involvement in Old Age* Erikson, Erikson, and Kivnick (1986) discuss the lack of employees over the age of 60 in a state department of aging. They note that when older people are hired, they tend to be used in routine or clerical capacities and "are all too regularly treated as clients or even patients in a kindly but deprecating way." There are many examples of older workers, often volunteers or part-time former skilled professionals, who are described as "special" or "cute." Ageism is not just a societal phenomenon; it exists within the very field of gerontology. Being aware of the existence of the problem is the first defense against it.

Even older professionals in the field sometimes harbor condescending and patronizing attitudes towards the elderly in general. I remember, for example, the director of the Family Service agency for which I worked who gave a passionate speech about how to deal with the elderly. "You have to understand these old people," she insisted. "You must recognize their needs!" This brisk, eloquent person, who spoke so protectively about the "old folks," was in her very late seventies. The last time I saw her, when she was 88, she reported to me with some anger that since I had left the agency she was having trouble with the old "fuddy-duddies," most of them in their fifties, who were "too old and set in their ways" to satisfy her. She retired, quietly, just before her ninetieth birthday because of a minor health problem; she did not consider her age, even then, to be at issue. And until that time it never occurred to her, or most of those who heard her, that anyone might mistake her for an old person. She was different!

An even more striking example of someone who dissociates himself from the elderly is to be found in a basic psychiatric text quoted by Butler and Lewis (1982). Alfred Noyes, an eminent psychiatrist, is quoted as saying:

> A dislike of change, a reduction in ambition and activity, a tendency to become constricted and self-centered in interests, an increased difficulty in comprehension, an increase in time and effort in adapting to new circumstances. . . . Many elderly people have little capacity to express warm and spontaneous feelings towards others. (p. 178)

As a young social work student in 1946, listening to a lecture by this same Dr. Noyes, I felt that he was really quite elderly. The quotation cited was written some 20 years later, when he must have been at least in his late sixties, so that he himself was of the age which he regarded in such unfavorable terms.

I do not believe that there is one of us, no matter what our age or professional orientation, who is totally free of bias or stereotypical thinking about aging and the elderly. I became acutely aware of this the day after my 65th birthday, when I found myself watching fellow passengers board a cruise ship and thinking, "But they're all so old!" Many of them were older than I was, but a livelier, more involved, and interesting group would be hard to imagine. I was truly ashamed of myself and could, after a while, say, "You know, they're looking at you and thinking the same thing!" The brighter side was that I could begin to look more critically and honestly at my own feelings. The resulting insight has enriched my practice as well as my personal life.

Throughout the professions, knowledge, skills, and ability are believed to reside in younger rather than older workers. And we older workers tend to go along with this assessment. We talk about how much simpler it was when we went to school, and how overwhelmed we are by "all this computer and high-tech stuff." We become vulnerable because of our own self-criticism. We downgrade our knowledge and skills even while we are busily attending conferences, taking courses, and becoming acquainted with our word processors. Far too often we defer to those whose knowledge is largely theoretical, and who therefore may interact infrequently with the objects of their study.

For example, in an informal discussion among gerontological counselors and care managers, I was interested when someone asked whether everyone thought it was necessary to be a parent to be a good parent-child counselor. The consensus was that it would be very hard to understand all the nuances of this relation-ship without firsthand knowledge. There was also a comment that working with substance abusers is best done by recovering abus-ers. But when I then asked whether one should therefore be elderly to work best with the elderly, there was a shocked silence. Not only did the younger people in the group find this "ridiculous" but the few older people who were there seemed very anxious to move on to another topic. I found it hard to see why my age peers seemed to deny the value of their firsthand knowledge of aging. All too often, however, we do. We become victims of our own ageism when we fail to use our ability to confront our own ambivalence, fears, and satisfactions about aging—our own countertransfer-ence issues.

Additionally, at this time service in the field of gerontological practice is still provided primarily by women. Age bias is compli-cated by sex bias. Lesnoff-Caravaglia (1984) comments that to be noticed, an older woman has to be an exceptional individual. She quoted Wilma Scott Heide, a former president of the National Organization of Women (NOW) who, in discussing public policy, says that gerontologists include few women. She adds that while they may talk to each other about older women, and may hold academic credentials, they still are likely to be experientially sex-ist, racist, ageist, classist, and homophobic. Melamed (1983) noted that as she interviewed older women she became acutely aware of "the discrepancy between our strengths and our minimal oppor-tunities to use them . . . as well as the damning fact that most of us accept these limitations as normal" (p. 15). The whole area of women's roles in gerontological practice looms large and bears further study.

On a more optimistic note, Dobrof (1987) commented on a conversation she had with the eminent geriatrician Robert Butler in which they acknowledged that they sometimes wished that they still had all their adult years to live.

> Having made this confession to each other—and both of us were, I think, somewhat chagrined at our vulnerability to this most human of frailties and yet relieved to find that it was a shared frailty—we talked about our hope that we and our colleagues in the field of aging would, in the years to come, be able to talk with candor and honesty about our own experience of aging. (page 4).

She goes on to make the very telling comment that "we observe our own aging and the aging of our peers—we clock our progress—and at the same time our ideology is a prism through which we make our observations (p. 4)."

Of course Dobrof, Butler and other leaders in the field of gerontology are to some degree protected from the institutional ageism that exists for the rank and file. It is unlikely that they have been told that they were "overqualified" (meaning too old to be useful) or that it was time to begin to think of themselves and take a well deserved rest. But Dobrof's willingness to look at and write about her own aging is encouraging. Perhaps recognizing often well-disguised bias against the elderly, even in gerontological practice, will make it possible for professionals to look at their own complex feelings in a more productive manner.

Making Use of Countertransference in Practice

Ageism influences the practitioner's personal life and professional skills. Understanding countertransference in this context can be very helpful. Practitioners who have accepted the fact of their own aging have identified both positive and negative feelings about aging, and have recognized the need to grapple with their own and their families' issues of aging, have the potential to relate better to the needs of their clients.

THE VALUE OF BEING OLDER

Older practitioners grapple with ageism in society, in the field of gerontology, and within themselves. But they also have distinct advantages that make it all worthwhile. An instance in which the value of being older was brought home to me occurred when I was convening a "Senior Rap Group" in which participants were reluctant to talk about their own feelings. One day I announced that the participants would no longer have to repeat themselves quite so often because I had, after much procrastination, finally gotten a hearing aid. Several members of the group thanked me, not only because I could openly admit that aging was causing me some problems, but because I could let them know how hard it had been for me to move ahead with them, how ambivalent I had been, and how I had tried to convince myself that the problem wasn't really that bad. As one of the members pointed out, anyone can wear glasses, but only old people wear hearing aids! This discussion led most members of the group to be much more open in discussing their own concerns. They began to talk about their resentment about the way most professionals talked to them and treated them "like children." The fact that I could identify my own feelings, and did not scold or lecture them allowed several group members to decide *independently* that it was all right for them, too, to use the aids they had been resisting. Hearing aids, canes, and even a walker appeared in the group. My admission of my own feelings about aging allowed me to work some things out for myself and freed the group members to trust and accept my ability to be helpful to them.

Unfortunately, many professionals run away from their own useful feelings. LeShan (1986) wrote that she was astonished when she was doing a survey of attitudes about aging to find professional people who refused to talk about their own feelings of aging, regarding this area as "too private to share." In the same vein, Melamed (1983) noted that as soon as she "confessed" to her own ambivalence about aging, there was a sudden change in the group, and women who had been reluctant to become involved were "quite willing to share, to stop being neutral and reticent." It sometimes takes courage to face our feelings of ageism, and to express them, but the rewards can be great, as illustrated by my work with Mr. Lesser.

I was asked to help Mr. Lesser plan for his return to the community from a nursing home. He is an emaciated, white haired man, wearing bedraggled oversized clothes. He walks slowly, talks vaguely and hesitantly. At first glance, I thought he must be at least ten or fifteen years older than I am. Actually, I learned that Mr. Lesser is only slightly older than I am, and that both our high school classes were holding their fiftieth reunions the very week we met. I had been doing a lot of thinking about what my classmates would look like, what they had accomplished, how many had died in the last half century, how I would appear to them. But I had to admit that it had never occurred to me that anyone of my generation could be so old and fragile. Here I was confronted with an unpleasant, indeed a frightening, picture of what my age could really mean. This made me very uncomfortable; I had to wonder whether I, too, could deteriorate so rapidly. My own feelings of ageism were becoming visible, and I was scarcely able to be helpful to Mr. Lesser while I was so anxious. It was only when I could face what we had in common that I became helpful to him. He showed the first signs of interest when I told him that we had impending class reunions in common.

As he talked about his school days, and then about his past in general, Mr. Lesser seemed to come to life. There was a two step process: first, I had to face seeing what someone my age who was "*really* old" meant to me. I had to come to terms with this for myself so that it would not impinge on the worker-client relationship. Second, Mr. Lesser began to see that someone his age could still function, plan and act, and he was able to search for the remaining strengths he did have. The coincidence of our ages showed me how imperative, and how effective, it was to look at my own countertransference issues in order to be able to work usefully with my client.

THE SIMULTANEOUS NEED FOR CONTROL AND CARE

With old people, who may appear to be crotchety and perverse, I find it important to recognize the two-way pull that comes with the awareness of changes caused by aging. For example, I can be quite disagreeable when someone tries to escort me out of a car or across a street; I often tell them testily that I can manage on my own with no difficulty. I am equally irked, however, when these same "helpful" people run ahead of me up a staircase or complete a sentence for me when I grope for the right word. When I mention my feelings about this to other older people, they relate strongly to my feeling about unasked for and unwanted assistance, and give their own examples of unsolicited and unwelcome help. Because I am aware of such changes in me, I can be much more patient with others who are also beginning to be forgetful, to move more carefully, and to deal with new and sometimes painful issues. What I might have seen earlier as contrariness or manipulation I now see as an effort to retain, if not independence, at least some degree of power. In both our personal and professional lives, we need not only independence and control, but also to be cared for and nurtured. And as we grow older, these needs are likely to co-exist all the more strikingly. They must be dealt with *not sequentially but simultaneously.* I am aware of my own need for certain accommodations because of my age, and of my need to control what kind of help I need and how I will use it. This enables me to empathize with similar feelings in my clients. This was illustrated by my work with Mrs. Willis, an 85-year-old, frail widow who lived alone, with no relatives nearby.

Several unsuccessful operations on her back had made walking very painful. Yet she consistently refused to allow anyone to help her, except for a casual friend who picked up her laundry every week. She agreed to counseling with me because we talked as adults and she did not feel that she was being patronized. She made it clear that it was all right for a friend to help her because this did not violate her feeling of being in control, but having an agency send in an aide would, she feared, "put them in charge." I was able to offer her the services of a companion whom she would pay directly, with the agency only providing initial placement and consultation if problems arose. She found this acceptable. Mrs. Willis feared that admitting her desperate need for help would result in interference with her right to control over her life. I was able to draw on my reserve of personal knowledge to help me recognize and empathize with her need to make choices.

At an earlier time, I might have reacted as another social worker did in a similar situation with Mrs. Mayer, also a widow living alone and unable to cope with all the details of her daily existence.

The social worker primarily worked with problems of young families; she was not familiar with many services for the elderly and believed that a nursing home was the only place where Mrs. Mayer could be "properly" cared for. However, she was unable to tell Mrs. Mayer this directly because this client reminded her of her grandmother, with whom she could never be authoritative. After she had spent many counseling sessions without achieving her goal, she decided to call in someone "older and wiser," saying quite frankly that she was "suffering from countertransference." In my first visit Mrs. Mayer made it very clear how much she wanted to remain at home. It was then possible to offer alternative plans, and she was able to choose an acceptable one. Mrs. Mayer needed assistance, but it had to be assistance that left her the greatest possible control. At first, all she claimed to need was a few hours of companion service twice a week; she herself gradually increased the time so that four years later the companion was on a full-time, 24-hour schedule. Mrs. Mayer remained at home, where she recently died with dignity and acceptance.

FAMILY SYSTEMS: THE CLIENT'S AND OUR OWN

Hooyman and Lustbader (1986) commented:

Professionals in the field of aging often feel especially neglectful about living a distance from their older relatives. In their daily work, they see the difference it makes when family members are actively involved in older people's lives. They tend to carry an extra degree of guilt about their own parents and grandparents: "Here I am helping everyone else's grandmother, while mine gets hardly any help from me." Such professionals are keenly aware of the difficulty of practicing their expertise over the phone or through brief visits. They also hear themselves giving advice to others that they are unable to follow in their own lives. For example, "How can I counsel other people to do what I'm not doing?" Furthermore, experienced helpers who are able to extrapolate from current circumstances to what the future is likely to bring for them do not have the luxury of ignorance about the implications of their choices. (p. 26)

The family system, whether our own family, client families, or the "organizational family," provides a fertile field for exploring countertransference and aging. Kirschner (1985) has pointed out that the counselor who thinks that an older person may be too fragile to be exposed to the interaction of family dynamics may have forgotten that this frail individual usually helped create and control these dynamics. Every member of every family is part of the problem and part of the solution.

If the practitioner is struggling with his or her own family relations, he or she may not be able to see what is going on. I recall a social worker in a family service agency who was in conflict with her sister over who should take care of their mother. She was assigned a case in which she was to assess a family where two sisters were locked in a similar conflict. The older sister complained that the younger had always been the favorite. The younger accused the older of using her greater financial resources to maintain control. In spite of the open conflict, the social worker reported that the two sisters got along beautifully! She could not see the client's family's arguments because she could not face her own conflict with her sister.

WHEN THE PROFESSIONAL NEEDS HELP

It is much easier for us to see when the client needs to take action than when we need to act ourselves. The supervisory conference is one obvious source of help. But there is no assurance that such help is always available. In many settings the whole concept of professional supervision and consultation is not recognized. Many supervisors are much younger than their supervisees, and this in itself may present countertransference problems—on both sides. Also, training in many therapeutic modalities emphasizes that a worker's personal problems do not belong in the supervisory relationship, so that other resources are needed. For example, a social worker who had been assigned a case dealing with a family's conflict about planning for their father could tell her supervisor that she was uncomfortable and wished that someone else could take over for her. She could not, however, say that a very similar battle was being waged in her own family, and that she was feeling very guilty. The family thought that her father should come to live with her because this was a daughter's role, but she did not want this to happen. She felt that this was a private and personal issue and none of the supervisor's business. Undoubtedly she also would have been embarrassed to have her colleagues know that she was not being a "good child." She tried very hard, but with little success, to help the client but her own feelings kept intruding until she finally could admit that she needed to do something about her own unresolved family situation. Although this case had to be transferred to another worker, at a later date, having resolved some of her own issues, she was able to work effectively with a similar situation.

Self-awareness and self-management are necessary to control responses to clients that have no helping value or are counterproductive (Greene, 1986). However, often it is not enough to "control" or "manage" countertransference reactions. For example, I may be angry at the need to disrupt my life to care for my ailing father. Even knowing how I feel, why I feel this way, and that I must separate my feeling from my client's feeling, may not be enough. I may need other assistance, in addition to good supervision and professional consultation. I may need therapy and access to social and health services, both to help myself and to find valuable insights that I can share with my clients.

I recall with some amusement a frantic telephone call I received from a highly experienced social worker who was herself close to retirement age. She was confronted with her father's medical and emotional crisis. She was paralyzed, and could not make any constructive move. I asked her whether she could help me with a case I was working on at the time she called, and described in specific detail what she had just told me. She was able to outline an assessment and care plan for this "unknown client" with no difficulty, but still did not realize that she was arriving at a plan for herself. She told me later that having been able to admit her need for help, and then having taken action instead of just agitating about it, was useful to her and had made her much more able to understand and work with clients.

In coping with such a universal phenomenon as aging, recognition of feelings and attitudes is only the starting point; what we *do* with our self-knowledge is critical. Assessing coping skills and support systems are merely preparation for action steps. "Do what I say, not what I do" just doesn't work, especially when dealing with mature, and often very wise, adults.

Dr. Edward Rosenbaum (1988) gave a dramatic example of what can happen, describing his experience as a patient, subjected to indignities, disdain, and lack of information. He strongly resented being given misleading, incomplete, and patronizing information, and resolved that he would never again be guilty of such behavior. Yet on his return to his medical practice he found that he was doing what he had always done, giving unrealistically cheerful information to a patient, thus depriving her of the right to make her own choices. We can hope that as he wrote about this, he was able to alter his style on his own, but I suspect that he would need to ask for help if he really intended to change. I would also hope that I, and my colleagues, would have the courage to ask for and use help in translating feelings into action.

KNOWING WHEN TO REVEAL FEELINGS

We need to be very aware of who we are, the kind of people we are, as much as we need to know who our clients are. Some of us are more comfortable with touching, crying, even laughing than others. Being able to be open about our own feelings can be very helpful. Most practitioners fear crying, seeing it as unprofessional, but being moved to tears can be significant. I worked with an older couple who, for medical and family reasons, moved back to the United States from Israel, where they had hoped to end their days. When they shared their sadness at having to give up something for which they had worked all their lives, my eyes filled with tears. They knew then that I could understand them.

Although our rich rainbow of feelings may be therapeutic for us, they may not always be relevant for our clients, their families, or our colleagues. We often need to seek consultation to come to terms both with what is really comfortable for us and what is appropriate in our work. For feelings to be used well, they must be genuine and must be dealt with within professional bound-aries. There is a fine line, not always easily established, between knowing when to use personal insights and illustrations in deal-ing with clients and when it is necessary to forego disclosure about ourselves and those with whom we are personally connected. I often tell stories about my mother to illustrate a point, but I would not discuss the guilt, the tensions in the family, the painful choices I had to make except under very special and clinically sound conditions.

Another common problem for me comes up in counseling older but still independent women who want to taper off the professional relationship and substitute personal friendship. This can be tempting, but it then becomes necessary to look at our own needs and personal resources before concluding that this might be appropriate; usually it is not. It is cruel to accept the friendship of a former client when we don't have the time or energy to sustain it. Although we may be less formal and more flexible with elderly clients, the professional relationship still has its boundaries.

Summary

There is no better way to understand the aging process, with its problems and rewards, than to grow old. All the academic and research knowledge in the world cannot fully help us through this uncharted and often surprising process. Much of what we learn can come from life experience, as long as we remain in close touch with our own feelings and behaviors, and recognize when we need help not only with personal feelings but with finding practical solutions to concrete problems. We cannot expect those with whom we work to get maximum benefit from our services, or even to accept the help we offer, if we have not come to terms with our own issues of aging, not just in theory but in practice.

Our feelings and attitudes are shaped and modified by many internal and external forces having to do with aging in America. We need to look carefully at the views of society as a whole, at the broad field of gerontological practice, and at how our attitudes have been influenced by these forces and by our own families. We need to catch ourselves when we indulge in stereotypical thinking and generalizing about the process of aging, both with ourselves and with our older clients and their families.

The older worker in gerontology has special personal knowledge, sensitivity, and expertise in aging. One of the most important insights we can provide is a deep understanding of older people's simultaneous need to retain independence and power while accepting increased assistance. Our self-awareness does not automatically translate into understanding of those with whom we are working, or into doing what we need to do about our own families' issues; continued training, supervision, consultation and positive action are necessary. One of the harsher myths about aging is that the elderly cannot learn. We know that this is not so and that the older practitioner, using a lifetime of knowledge and experience, continues to learn and grow. When we use the totality of our own feelings, the contribution of the older practitioner is not only meaningful but of extraordinary value.

References

Butler, R. N., & Lewis, M. (1982). *Aging and mental health* (3rd ed.) (p. 178). St. Louis: C. V. Mosby.

Dobrof, R. (1987). The aging of a gerontologist. *Pride Institute Journal, 6,* 4.

Erikson, E. H., Erikson, J. M., & Kivnick, H. (1986). *Vital involvement in old age.* New York: Norton.

Greene, R. (1986). Countertransference issues in social work with the aged. *Journal of Gerontological Social Work, 9*(3), 79-88.

Hooyman, N. R., & Lustbader, W. (1986). *Taking care* (p. 26). New York: Free Press.

Kirschner, C. (1985). Social work practice with the aged and their families: A systems approach. *Journal of Gerontological Social Work, 8*(3/4), 55-67.

Knight, R. (1986). *Psychotherapy with older adults.* Beverly Hills, CA: Sage.

LeShan, E. (1986). *Oh to be 50 again!* New York: Times Books.

Lesnoff-Caravaglia, G. (Ed.). (1984). *The world of the older woman.* New York: Human Sciences Press.

Melamed, E. (1983). *Mirror, mirror: The terror of not being young.* New York: Simon & Schuster.

Meyer, C. (Ed.). (1986). *Social work with the aging.* Silver Spring, MD: National Association of Social Workers.

Rosenbaum, E. (1988). *A taste of my own medicine.* New York: Random House.

13

Facing the Challenge: Weaving Countertransference Feelings into the Tapestry of Our Work

RENÉE S. KATZ

Countertransference is often ignored, overlooked, or concealed, but it is an essential part of gerontology practice. Professional training across disciplines seems to have actually encouraged a lack of awareness of personal-professional connections by emphasizing client objectivity, professional distance, and intellectual understanding—at the expense of emotional understanding (Tansey & Burke, 1985). In practice, however, it is not always clear whether our actions on behalf of our clients and families are based on truly objective professional judgments or whether they are based in part on our concepts of and confrontations with aging and aging family members in our own lives (Greene, 1986).

Like older people, gerontologists themselves cope with aging, disability, loss, and grief. And, like older people, helping professionals come from, are involved in, and are affected by their families of origin and their current family lives.

Our relationships with parents, siblings, grandparents, and other older loved ones shape our attitudes and coping styles (Weiner, 1989), our self-concepts and biases. We inevitably bring these personality styles and relationship histories into each new relationship and into each new experience. When our own aging processes and developmental tasks intermix with those of our families and the people we work with, we may find that an emotional "pressure point" is activated. An emotional reaction—a personal, professional, and familial connection—is triggered. The results are often intense feelings and behaviors. These countertransference reactions may dumbfound us, surprise us, shock us, or delight us! If we face them, they will inform us, and improve our practice.

Facing the Issues

This book has attempted to address countertransference feelings so that we as practitioners can help our clients face aging, loss, disability, and death with dignity and integrity, with power and choice. The authors of this book have named our most common countertransference reactions: anger and resentment; inadequacy and failure; powerlessness and lack of control; frustration and guilt; sadness and grief; fears of aging, emotional pain, losses, dependency and death. If we ignore, defend against, or distance ourselves from these emotional reactions, we run the risk of "helping" clients and patients back *into* the very problem areas for which they have consulted us (see Table 13.1).

Implications for Practice

In our training as gerontologists, we are encouraged to identify, dispute, defy, even rage against societal ageism. (Levin & Levin, 1980). Occasionally, we might be encouraged to look at attitudes about aging which we have learned from our families of origin.

Table 13.1 Countertransference Problem Areas with Older Clients

Client behavior	Helper's feeling response	Manifestations in helper's behaviors	Effects on client
Refuses services, makes "unrealistic" demands—with demonstrated resentment, anger, hostility, emotional lability	Inadequate, useless, sense of failure—with underlying anger, resentment	*Overidentification:* Feels guilty about own anger, overcompensates, works beyond the call of duty, wishes the client would terminate, loses objectivity, imposes personal beliefs on client, forces disclosure of information, retaliates	Exacerbates feelings of anger, emotional lability; client feels misunderstood, increases demanding behavior or refuses service
		Distortion: Overlooks client needs and fears, expects too much or too little, withdraws support, prematurely discharges the client, questions own competencies, feels smug about an intervention that is actually inappropriate, portrays clients as far worse than they are	
Constant phone calls, lack of confidence in own skills, pulls for more help, dependency—with demonstrated fear, panic, anxiety, agitation	Powerless, out-of-control, helpless—with underlying fear of the unknown, own aging, losses, disability, emotional pain, abandonment, helplessness, dependency, or death	*Projection:* Blames the client or family for problems, becomes parental in approach, overinterprets everything as a crisis, encourages premature or tardy placement, structures interventions too rigidly; over- or underemphasizes client issues	Exacerbates fears, sense of powerlessness, dependency, abandonment; client may not receive appropriate level of care, may submit to helplessness, or feel rejected
		Rationalization: Makes excuses, denies severity of problems, "protects" client from diagnosis or prognosis "for their own good," finds reasons for inappropriate interventions, produces too many concrete, practical suggestions rather than dealing with feelings	

(Continued)

185

Table 13.1 (Continued)

Client behavior	Helper's feeling response	Manifestations in helper's behaviors	Effects on client
Lack of motivation, expresses suicidal thoughts—with demonstrated grief, loss, depression	Vulnerable, despairing, devastated—with underlying sadness, grief, depression, or suicidal thoughts	*Denial:* Avoids issues that generate emotional pain, inaccurately assesses situations, denies expression of feelings; interrupts, avoids, or terminates service, fails to schedule appointments, reduces opportunities for grief work, rushes or hurries visits and phone calls, colludes with client to minimize the extent of losses and changes	Exacerbates feelings of sadness and loss, vulnerability; client loses faith in the helping system, may return to suicidal thoughts, may manipulate the helper into action
Confusion, immobilization, ambivalence	Desperate, frustrated, disgusted—with underlying guilt or inappropriate sense of responsibility for client	*Displacement:* Displaces own family issues onto the client, overlooks other pressing needs or problems, decides for the client what his or her "real" problem is, acts oversolicitous, paternalistic	Exacerbates client's confusion, apathy, frustration; client feels misunderstood, alone with feelings, submits to helplessness
		Reaction Formation: Portrays false optimism, appears competent and cheery, minimizes client's feelings, acts bored, becomes apathetic	

Table 13.2 Early Behavioral Signals of Countertransference

Feeling intense emotional reactions or unusual feelings (e.g., feeling intensely angry, demeaned, vulnerable, devastated, "shook to the core," manipulated, drained, irritated)

Forgetting appointments

Losing patience

Feeling sleepy, bored, unable to concentrate

Intervening beyond the call of duty

Giving poorer attention or care or denying service completely

Attempting to persuade or convince a client or family about your viewpoint—at any cost

Arguing for no good reason

Avoiding a client or family

Trying to transfer a client or family

Wishing the client or family would drop out or seek services elsewhere

---

But *rarely* are we encouraged to look at our *own* concepts of aging as they are confronted and challenged by the people with whom we work and by the disruptions in our own lives. Rarely are we encouraged to examine our own behaviors in response to clients— clues that countertransference may be astir (see Table 13.2).

Identifying situations that "hook" us, examining our behaviors, and recognizing feelings we have been trained *not* to have is crucial. Supervision, professional support groups, in-service education, training, consultation, and sometimes individual or group therapy are necessary in order to work through countertransference feelings. The most effective training allows professionals to connect ageism, fears of dying and disability, and personal issues of loss in their own families with their current beliefs about aging, grieving, and resolution of family issues. Confrontation of personal and professional fears of failure, analysis of our need for control in the face of loss, facilitation of unresolved grief work, and clarification of beliefs about professional competency as they relate to feelings of personal responsibility and guilt are critical stepping stones along the path to identifying the sources of countertransference reactions.

If we can acknowledge personal feelings triggered in professional encounters, even if they initially seem inappropriate or unacceptable, we can put countertransference feelings to work in the service of clients. Understanding our own feelings enhances our understanding of our clients' experiences and gives us important clues to what may be happening in our interactions with them. We can then use these clues. By our tone of voice, our facial expression and our very presence, we can demonstrate our capacity to tolerate the uncomfortable feelings and situations that our clients experience. We can use countertransferential feelings as tools to communicate what we empathically understand—sometimes all too well! Then we can actualize this countertransference potential, formulating appropriate strategies and plans based on deeper and more accurate understanding of our clients' and families' experiences.

Summary

The practitioner needs to become aware of what kinds of clients bring out his/her negative [countertransference] responses as well as what "special vulnerabilities" he/she brings to the therapeutic encounter. . . . When countertransference feelings are displaced onto the client, the . . . [helper] is no longer able to effectively hold the position of listener, observer, discussant, thinker and outsider. The sense of professional objectivity is diminished as is the ability to perceive . . . the client's needs. (Greene, 1989, pp. 86-87)

Countertransference provides an extraordinary opportunity for the helping person to look at his or her own distance from potential and real loss, disability, and death in order to be a more competent helper. As gerontology professionals, we can choose to confront and identify the sources of our emotional pressure points—our countertransference reactions—or we can deny them. If we deny countertransference feelings, we may be less helpful to the individuals and families who activate these feelings in us. If we acknowledge these feelings, we can refine our skills and weave them meaningfully into the tapestry of our work. The key lies in our abilities to be honest about our feelings so that we can use them as empathic bridges in our client-helper relationships.

References

Greene, R. R. (1986, Spring). Countertransference issues in social work with the aged. *Journal of Gerontological Social Work, 9*(3), 79-88.

Katz, R. S., & Genevay, B. (1987, Spring). Countertransference, older people and dying: The personal-professional connection. *Generations, 3*(11), 28-32.

Levin, J., & Levin, W. C. (1980). *Ageism: Prejudice and discrimination against the elderly.* Belmont, CA: Wadsworth.

Tansey, M. H., & Burke, W. F. (1985). Projective identification and the empathic process. *Contemporary Psychoanalysis, 21*(1), 42-69.

Weiner, I. B. (1989). Family therapists have family too. *Contemporary Psychology, 34*(12), 1141.

About the Authors

Patrick Arbore is Director of Geriatric and Grief Programs of San Francisco Suicide Prevention, Inc. He is also a doctoral student in Counseling and Educational Psychology at the University of San Francisco and a part-time faculty member of the College of Notre Dame, Belmont, California.

Louise Bernstein, A.C.S.W., C.I.S.W., is current President of Elder Family Service of Connecticut, a private counseling and care management organization that serves the elderly and their families. She has over 44 years of professional social work experience, having worked in psychiatric settings, served as regional director of a family service agency for 15 years, and directed a funded, large case-management agency for seven years.

Susan DelMaestro, Ph.D., was formerly a psychotherapist at the Stanford University School of Medicine Older Adult and Family Center. She currently is Staff Psychologist at the Philadelphia Veterans Administration Medical Center.

Bonnie Genevay, M.S.W., Ph.D., is a nationally known trainer and consultant in gerontology and bereavement, a part-time faculty member of Family Service American Western Regional Institute, and serves as a consultant to hospice and home health agencies. She has worked with universities, hospitals, gerontology associations, agencies, retirement and nursing homes, and state divisions on aging since 1973. She has served on the board of directors of the American Society on Aging, has been a trainer for the organization for many years, and currently serves on the editorial board of *Generations*, the journal of the society. She is author of numerous articles and chapters on loss and grief, intimacy in late life, the aging family, and counseling older people. For 16 years she has been on the staff of Family Services in Seattle, Washington, as a therapist, supervisor, trainer, and director of their aging services program.

Edith S. Kaplan, M.S.W. and diplomate in Clinical Social Work, is a psychotherapist in private practice and Clinical Staff Member at the University of California, San Francisco Memory Clinic and Alzheimer Center.

Renée S. Katz, M.S.W., is Clinical Psychologist and Diplomate in Clinical Social Work in private practice in San Francisco and Menlo Park, California. She is Faculty Member of San Francisco State University and formerly was outpatient Psychotherapist at Stanford University Medical Center, Department of Psychiatry. She now devotes most of her time to providing counseling and consultation to individuals and couples, groups, community professionals, and agencies. She has published and presented seminars nationally on issues including gerontology, trauma, grief and loss, chemical dependency, and stress-related disorders.

Maureen O'Neil, M.S.W., is a licensed clinical social worker. Employed by San Mateo County Mental Health Department, she works in the HIV Early Intervention Program. She is also Clinical Consultant with ELLIPSE Peninsula AIDS Services and Group Facilitator with Alzheimer's Disease and Related Disorder Association, Palo Alto, California.

Jeanne Robinson, M.S., is a gerontologist with a private practice in the San Francisco Bay Area. Through employers and individual family consultation, she helps working people learn how to manage the care of their frail elderly loved ones. She also provides social work services in independent senior housing. Her business, Third Age, is based in San Francisco.

Marvin L. Rosenberg, Jr., M.S.S.W., is a Board Certified Diplomate in clinical social work, and since 1980 has been a member of the Academy of Certified Social Workers. He is currently an adult therapist specializing in geriatrics and a Senior Peer Counseling Program Director at Group Health Cooperative of Puget Sound. He maintains a private practice and is an adjunct faculty member in the Psychology Department at Antioch University in Seattle.

Martha Sebastian-Moyer, M.S.W., L.C.S.W., is Director of the Amyotrophic Lateral Sclerosis Association of Los Angeles and Instructor in the Graduate School of Social Work of California State University, Long Beach. A psychotherapist, she conducts training seminars on countertransference and other issues related to working with older adults for professionals around the country.

Irene Williams, M.S.W., A.C.S.W., is Family Consultant/Case Manager with the Del Oro Regional Resource Center, a nonprofit agency, which is part of a statewide system of resource centers serving family caregivers of brain-impaired adults. Following several years as a family therapist and part-time instructor, notably at the UCLA Extension School of Social Work, she became Coordinator of the behavioral science component in family medicine at Riverside General Hospital in Riverside, California, and later developed a peer counseling and outreach program for the elderly in Sacramento, California.